THE QUEEN OF GRANTS
FROM TEACHER TO GRANT WRITER TO CEO

LIBBY HIKIND

All rights reserved.

Hardcover ISBN: 979-8-218-35793-1
Paperback ISBM: 979-8-218-35794-8

Disclaimer

The use of this book implies your acceptance of this disclaimer. GrantWatch, the publisher and Libby Hikind, the author, make no guarantees concerning the level of success you may experience by following the advice and strategies in this book, and you accept the understanding that results will differ for each individual and/or organization.

Copyright © 2024 GRANTWATCH
First paperback edition February 1, 2024.

All rights reserved. No part of this book may be reproduced or used in any manner without the prior written permission of the copyright owner, except for the use of brief quotations in a book review. To request permissions, contact the publisher at support@grantwatch.com

GRANTWATCH
PO Box 742911
Boynton Beach, FL 33437
Printed by GRANTWATCH in the USA.

GrantWatch is a secure search and listing directory of currently available grants accepting grant applications. GrantWatch does not give grants. Never pay an imposter who asks you to pre-pay money or send a wire or gift card for a guaranteed grant or money back.

Testimonials

"Libby Hikind, First in Her Name, Matriarch of Parchment, Sovereign of Submissions, Defender of All Documents, Weaver of Words, Guardian of Grants, and Steward of the Sanctum of Strategic Storytelling has finally written, and shares with all of her fundraising subjects, glorious tips and tricks on how to write like the Queen of Grants she is!

There is no one who quite makes the process clearer and more concise, and Libby is one of the most brilliant minds when it comes to developing, executing, and managing grants. Long Live the Queen!" **-Patrick Kirby, Author of "Fundraise Awesomer! A Practical Guide to Staying Sane While Doing Good"**

"Thank you for this book, Libby. There are a lot of books written about Grants, but very few have been written by someone with your expertise and with a genuine goal of enlightening charitable organizations around the world. Your act of selflessness will reverberate in the United States, in Latin America, Africa and around the entire globe. We will continue to invite you to our events, especially now that you have finally written your book which has been years in the making." **-Donna Y Scantlebury MBA, Florida State Representative for Sister Cities International**

"Libby Hikind, the visionary Founder of GrantWatch, has not only revolutionized the world of grants but has also shared her invaluable insights in this book. Her expertise and dedication to the grant community shine through every page. The book is a testament to Libby's passion for empowering individuals and organizations through grant opportunities. A must-read for anyone navigating the grant landscape, as Libby's wisdom is a guiding light in the pursuit of funding for impactful projects."**-Jason R. Hill, Founder of "Owwll" and Host of "The Shrimp Tank"**

"As a seasoned grant writer for 30 years, I am so grateful for Libby Hikind's insight. I personally can attest to her mentorship throughout my tenure. Her book encapsulates all the mentorship and wisdom that guides those seeking to learn how to write grants. She is the 'Queen of Grants', and while she may now be a CEO ... Libby is forever a teacher.

Successful grant applications are not just about writing skill — there is a psyche that must be understood between the client and the funder. Libby shares her tools of the trade that only she truly possesses. I encourage those at the beginning stage of their career to the most experienced to please read every word. There is something to learn for all." **-Marsha Jaquays, CEO of Grant Whiz LLC.**

"Libby is a true leader in the field of grant writing, having mastered the art of successful grant applications. Her expertise and simple approach to grant writing have made her a valuable resource for individuals and organizations seeking funding for their projects.

Her ability to simplify the often daunting and complex process, making it accessible to all. She has a talent for breaking down the process into manageable steps, guiding others through each stage with ease and clarity." **-Duvi Honig, Founder and Chief Executive Officer, Orthodox Jewish Chamber of Commerce**

"Libby Hikind is a consummate professional who has taken her natural talents and honed them into enormous skills and immense success in Grant Writing. A professional of unparalleled caliber, she not only delivers expertise to her clients but is gracious enough, through this book, to share her talents and decades of triumphant experience with others. Anyone interested in grants would do well to heed her advice, formula, and instruction on how to be successful in a field where few have the successful track record that Libby can boast." **-David Beryl Phillips, Attorney at Law, and Former Campaign Manager for Libby's NYC Council race.**

Dedication

This book is dedicated to the memory of my parents, Hannah and Tovia. My parents taught me through their good deeds, actions, and involvement in the nonprofit sector. Their memory continues to this day, to be an integral part of my strength, knowledge, devotion, and work ethic.

This book is dedicated to my GrantWatch family, staff, and subscribers, and my daughter Lani, my unofficial business partner, my springboard, my rock, and my friend.

This book is dedicated to my husband Jacob, my daughter Lianne, and my cousin Sue who have encouraged me to leave this legacy for future generations of grant writers.

This book is also dedicated to my children Erica, Elliot, and Elissa for their contributions along the way, their patience with a self-driven mother, and everyone who has encouraged me throughout my life's journey.

LIBBY HIKIND

LEARN FROM THE CEO OF GRANTWATCH.COM

TESTIMONIALS III

DEDICATION V

FORWARD 13

    It Is a True Honor, Thank You! 13

PROLOGUE 17

    Inch by Inch, Life's A Cinch 17

I: HOW IT ALL BEGAN FOR ME 19

    A teacher in need of a solution. 20
    I was determined to be effective. 23
    My first grant. 24
    Lessons not learned. 25
    This was the beginning of my grant writing career. 29
    Beating the odds with curriculum. 30
    Not getting the job. 32
    Educational admin: grant writer at the district office. 33
    A sampling of the grants I wrote and won, at the DO. 36
    The youth gang grant. 37

Life was stressful. 40

Opening my own grant writing business. 42

Writing curriculum. 44

Running for city council. 45

Primary Day, 9/11 Attack on World Trade Center. 47

My team of first responders. 49

My three angels. 51

Child Health Plus: The grant that kept on giving. 54

Project Liberty hired me, after 9/11. 55

I returned to teaching when the school year started. 58

I retired from teaching and found my artsy side. 59

More than anyone, I understood the need. 61

The start of GrantWatch. 63

Reviewing grants for the federal government. 69

We expanded the reach of the website. 70

The start of GrantWatch.com 71

A life of building blocks. 84

Personal attention created our solid foundation. 85

Challenges of a website. 87

What I would tell my younger self. 89

I was still writing grants. 90

Why did I create GrantWriterTeam? 92

Teaching Grant Writing and Public Speaking 93

The start and sale of YouHelp.com 97

Work-life balance 98

My advice to entrepreneurs. 100

The last straw for GrantWriterTeam 105

We developed a new business model for GrantWriterTeam. 109

GrantWriterTeam is not a money-making website. 110

II: YOUR QUESTIONS ANSWERED 113

What is a grant? 113
How do I receive a grant? 114
Where do grants come from? 115
Do I have to pay back a grant? 116
Can I include a grant writer's salary in the budget? 119
Is it difficult to apply for grants? 122
How to avoid grant scams? 123
What are the 990s? 124
What 990 information is helpful? 126
How long does it take to write a grant? 128
How much does it cost to hire a grant writer? 129
Should I hire a grant writer? 133
Can you apply for grants while your IRS tax-exempt status is pending? 134
Are there grants for small businesses? 134
Should we become a charity? 137
How did COVID-19 affect grant funding? 139
How are federal grants scored? 140
How are foundation grants scored? 142
Why should we apply for a particular grant? 142
When will I be notified if I win a grant? 143
Is it easier to apply for a foundation grant than a government grant? .. 145
What is the likelihood of your proposal being funded? 146
How can I maximize our chances of success? 147
What are my options if my grant proposal is rejected? 147
What do I do with my rejected grant proposal? 148
How can I obtain reviewers' notes and scores given to my application? 148
What is an LOI, letter of intent? 149
What range of monetary grants are available? 151

How many grants can companies apply for at the same time? 152
How much does it cost to be a GrantWatch subscriber?......................... 153
Do private foundations receive grants?... 154

III: HOW TO WRITE A GRANT? 155

ELIGIBILITY 157

Review a funder's 990 to determine your likelihood of getting funded... 161
When fiscal sponsorship is needed. 163

FOLLOW DIRECTIONS 169

Federal grant formatting guidelines.. 172

PMF: PASSION, MAPS AND FOLDERS 175

WHY DID I CREATE THE MNEMONIC, PMF? 176

PASSION... 177

Passion, Partnerships and Consortiums... 178

MAPS 180

Your elevator pitch. 184
Writing an LOI. 185
Needs... 188
Goals.. 192
Measurable objectives – outcomes 192
Activities 194
Timelines.. 194
Evaluation.. 197
Evaluation Consultant 199
Budget 200
Table of organization... 205
Management of grant funds 206

Staffing 207

FOLDERS **208**

Folders of Legal & Registrations 210

Folder of Community Needs Data 212

Folder of Organizational Support 213

Folder of Organizational Capacity & Strengths 214

Folder of Fiscal Management 216

YOU WON!!! CELEBRATE **217**

Grant award - confirm all the details. 217

Open a separate bank account. 218

Your grant award will not be private. 219

Next steps 219

Budget modifications 219

Audits, reports, and progress 221

Keep a hard copy and an electronic copy. 222

Meet the deadlines the funding source sets. 222

Achieve, achieve, achieve. 223

Review your results. 223

SUSTAINABILITY **224**

DISSEMINATION – SHARING **226**

Have you won a grant that you found on GrantWatch? 228

REPLICABILITY **230**

IV: MODELING SUCCESSFUL GRANTS **233**

Modeling the mapping process. 233

Stats to Include in a Needs Section 241

Sample Needs to Include 241

Examples of Goals Section 244

Needs Assessment and Your Hook 246

Tell a Captivating Story 247

Example of a Hook 250

Example of Needs Section 252

Example of Activities Section 254

Example of Evaluation Section 256

Example of Organizational Capacity Section 257

Examples of Timelines Section 260

Example of Budget Section 264

Example of Fiscal Management Section 272

Examples of Tables of Organization 276

Table of Organization Samples 278

Example of a Letter of Inquiry 281

V: THE FUTURE OF AI AND GRANT WRITING 285

How I prompted ChatGPT to write a sample LOI 286

An LOI, letter of intent or inquiry written with AI 288

The use of AI, Artificial Intelligence 292

My book is ending, and your story is beginning 294

ABOUT THE AUTHOR 297

ACKNOWLEDGMENTS 299

FORWARD

It Is a True Honor, Thank You!

I am honored that you have chosen my book to mentor you through the grant writing process. The Queen of Grants from Teacher to Grant Writer to CEO will take you on my journey, answer all your questions about grant writing and then show you the components of a grant and provide some writing samples. At the end of the book, we will start to explore the ethical place of AI in the grant writing process.

I want to take you step by step through the grant process, teaching you what is most important to know and do, in order to complete a winning grant application, and for you (yes, YOU), to write your best grant proposal, ever!

My goal is for you to believe, "I can do it too!" by sharing my journey from public school teacher to grant writer, to founder and CEO of GrantWatch.com.

Many, many years ago, as a young special education classroom teacher I felt the intimidation and insecurity most people feel when staring at a grant application. I was unprepared for the task, asking myself, "How will I write this grant?" There were no "How-to Books" on grant writing that I could access, and Google had not yet been created.

Still, I was extremely fortunate. School Principal, Nat Rothman and Deputy Superintendent and Director of Grants, Phyllis Gonon took me under their wings. I became their very own pet project. They provided valuable guidance and encouragement and I learned so much from them that I was able to write my first grant, and win!

In September 2021, I was featured on The Shrimp Tank podcast, conducted in collaboration with the FAU, Florida Atlantic University Adams Center for Entrepreneurship. The moderator Host, Jason R. Hill, introduced me as *The Queen of Grants.* I asked him why and he said, "Because you, Libby, have the most extensive grant background and have also experienced grants through the eyes of an applicant, an awardee, a peer reviewer, a researcher, and a public speaker."

I loved my new identity and was grateful to be recognized for my achievements. He validated my desire to write a book and so I revisited the book outline, I had started in March of that year.

In August 2022, Patrick Kirby introduced me the same way on his, Do Good Better Podcast. He called the segment, Lessons From "*The Queen of Grants*" Libby Hikind. I chatted with

Patrick afterward about his experience publishing his book, and together, we bounced around titles for my book.

I have divided my book into 5 sections, each of which can be read independently or altogether in its entirety.

    I.   How It All Began for Me
    II.   Your Questions Answered
    III.   How To Write a Grant?
    IV.   Modeling Successful Grants
    V.   The Future of AI and Grant Writing

I hope, through my book, *The Queen of Grants: From Teacher to Grant Writer to CEO,* you too can see grants as I do and get funded. When you feel you have honed this craft, please pay the book forward, and pass it on.

LIBBY HIKIND

PROLOGUE

Inch by Inch, Life's A Cinch

One day, I got a message from my staff that an acquaintance of mine was trying to reach me. It was the Wednesday before Thanksgiving, and I returned the call.

We spoke for about 30 minutes. My "blast from the past," acquaintance wanted to become a grant writer. She is currently a business coach and has persuasive writing experience and skills. I thought she'd make a fine grant writer.

While schmoozing, I told her to watch the podcasts under the Media tab on my website. I apologized that my book *The Queen of Grants: from Teacher to Grant Writer to CEO* wasn't out yet, but I did have 250 first draft pages already written. I shared with her that I keep beating myself up (in my mind) for lacking the discipline to write for one hour a day. My last entry was exactly 3 months ago.

She then shared her mantra with me, and I got the best advice ever, "Yard by yard, life is hard, but inch by inch, life's a cinch."

On Thanksgiving morning, I felt forever grateful to Jeanie because there I was, with 11 people coming for Thanksgiving dinner, still writing for more than an hour, with only the expectation of accomplishing an inch.

One Sunday in early December, The Hallmark Channel previewed one of those corny holiday movies we all love to watch. This one, *Round and Round* was about a person stuck in a time loop with a draft of her first sci-fi manuscript hidden in a box in her childhood room.

Forget the romantic comedy plot, I zeroed in on her book. My take from the movie was that her book remained unedited and not published due to fear of rejection. The proverbial light bulb went on in my head seeing the three people she trusted editing and re-editing her book throughout the time loop.

On Monday morning I woke up, confided in the GrantWatch editor Lori that I had authored a book. She was more than thrilled! Her excitement about editing my book added trust. I felt the comfort level I needed to put my book in her hands. Lori was to be my first read. Next it would go to family, staff, and friends. We set a deadline for the final draft manuscript by December 31, 2023. My book was then published thirty-one days later on February 1, 2024.

If you are going round and round, stuck in a loop, it's not necessarily procrastination or laziness. Assess what you're afraid of and address it by taking that very first step. After all, "Inch by inch, life's a cinch."

I: How It All Began For Me

My name is Libby Hikind, and this is my journey. I started my career in education at age 15 as a Sunday school teacher. By seventeen, I was teaching preschool. I later became a paraprofessional, while student teaching. I also taught grade 5 in a private school, and by the age of twenty-five, I was a certified teacher for the NYC Department of Education.

I wrote and won my first grant while employed at the NYC Department of Education, teaching, at what was then a junior high school, special education class (grades 7-9).

Today, I am the founder and CEO of GrantWatch.com, the leading grant funding website.

Before you decide to take any kind of grant writing instruction or mentoring from me, I want to share my story with you and explain my background and what led me to the world of grant writing and into the role of CEO.

A teacher in need of a solution.

My grant writing career started all the way back when I was teaching a special education class at a junior high in Brooklyn, New York. At that time, my highest level of education was a bachelor's degree in elementary education with a minor in fine arts. (I later went on to get my master's in special education and a post graduate certificate in educational administration and supervision.)

At that time, I admit I was ill-equipped to teach a special education class. However, as a parent of two young children, securing any city position with the benefits and hours being offered was my dream job.

In hindsight, it's understandable that the position I was being offered, after calling every week that summer, was the only teaching job still available on the Friday before the 1978-79 school term.

I had to drop my kids off at a neighbor's house and get myself to headquarters and complete the paperwork all in one day.

In the olden days, or some might say the "golden days," the school nurse could not administer prescribed psychotropic medicines (the norm at the time) to students during the school day. My classroom of 10 children was called CEH, a Class for the Emotionally Handicapped. That was the term in those days, not appropriate today, but that was the classification then. Years later they relabeled my classroom MIS II. (MIS I was learning disabled).

I always had a full-time paraprofessional (para, for short) in my classroom. Thankfully, my para was an over 6-foot-tall male (or it seemed so at the time). I had a false sense of security within the walls of the classroom.

So, there were 10 students, a paraprofessional, me, and a landline telephone to call for help. At the time, the medical industry and the school system were still unsure how to treat severely emotionally disabled students. The school did not administer prescribed medications and acting out was common.

To give you some background, it was the late 1970s and early 1980s, and it was before the widespread use of Ritalin. It was also just a few years after Willowbrook the (infamous New York state-run school for children with intellectual disabilities) and other such facilities were shuttered.

Because of advances in special education, a few years later, all special ed students were mandated by the Department of Education to take the same writing exams as the mainstream student population.

My students had far to go to improve their writing skills. If I recall correctly, they needed to write a persuasive business letter, an essay, and a how-to article.

All my students were overly sensitive to negative comments. If I made a single correction on their paper or even offered a verbal suggestion, they would just crumple their work into a ball and throw it at me.

What to do? What to do? I had to find a way to make writing and editing enjoyable. I started reading educational periodicals about word processing to learn how to incorporate the use of computers in the classroom. I knew that my school had a small experimental computer lab, and I believed this would be a welcome addition.

So, I went to the school principal, and after much discussion about the highly valuable computers, he said yes, but I would need to educate myself and learn enough about computers to stay ahead of my students. He scheduled the time for my class in the computer lab.

I found that the school computers did not have enough memory for word processing. However, I was able to learn BASIC programming language and proceeded to teach my students to write simple programs to make things move across the screen, calculate math problems, and pick lottery numbers randomly.

Remember, this was the early '80s, and desktop computers were just beginning to make their way into schools. What my students were able to accomplish was nothing short of amazing. And they were more cooperative, and I think it was because they enjoyed our computer lab time.

Still, I was disappointed with the capability of our computer lab because the computers lacked enough memory and other components needed for word processing.

We wanted to use the computers to teach writing skills, and I wasn't ready to give up on that idea. The upcoming writing exam was looming large and the need to prepare my special ed students was at the top of my mind.

I was determined to be effective.

I met with Alan Sebel, my special education supervisor, and expressed my disappointment with the computer capacity at our school and he suggested I put together a word processing equipment list and a budget of what would be needed.

Alan was going to bring it to the local Community School District office. We were both confident that we were going to get the funds needed because, in those years, large sums of money were being thrown into special education.

To our surprise, the school district said they didn't have the money to allocate for my classroom.

My first grant.

The school district gave a mixed response: they said no due to a lack of funds, but also yes, as there was a grant available from Tandy Corporation, the parent company of Radio Shack.

Community School District 18 had applied for a grant from Tandy in a previous cycle but did not win. With the no, they also sent this message to me, through Alan, "If Libby is willing to come every day after school, we are willing to teach her how to write a grant."

I did just that. I needed to pay for extra after-school babysitting services for my own children, but I was given an opportunity to learn, and I was going to put in the effort.

Thanks to the grant writers and the deputy superintendent at Community School District 18, I learned how to write a grant.

Tandy Corporation was offering computer equipment to 4 schools or nonprofits that could demonstrate how the Tandy Model 100 could be used in an educational environment.

FIGURE 1: THE MODEL 100 WAS PROBABLY ONE OF THE FIRST TABLETS EVER, WITH A 4-INCH GREEN SCREEN AND A PHYSICAL KEYBOARD.

Lessons not learned.

I made two exceptionally large mistakes. Most days, after school, I was either at the district office or meeting with my school principal, Mr. Nat Rothman. He encouraged my writing and reviewed what I would be obligating the school to in the grant application.

At night, after putting my children to bed, I taught myself how to use a Commodore 64 and Bank Street Writer, a user-friendly word-processing program. I had only mastered the Commodore 64 a few days before I began writing the grant proposal. Learning about word processing was a revelation; it saved me from the tedious cycle of typing, erasing, and retyping, which I had always disliked.

There was a small detail I did not learn from my mentors, and I missed it in the computer manual. I did not realize that you needed to save your work and save it often. When I crossed my legs under my writing desk at home, I kicked out the computer plug, and I lost all 23 pages of what I had written.

I had so much drive and passion for what I wanted to accomplish, that I rewrote the entire proposal and probably had a better piece of writing the second time around.

My second major blunder was that, while I proofread my grant, I did not know about the spell check feature. All of this is second nature to everyone today. But then again, the only people in my community that knew computers at that time worked on large mainframes. When I shared with my friends what I was discovering, it was more like, "Libby, can you please speak English?"

After making the required copies and mailing the physical application to Tandy (Radio Shack), I sat down to pat myself on the back and reread my grant. That's when I realized that I had missed many typos.

I was devastated and started to cry. When I composed myself, I called the funding source. I was so embarrassed by the typos that I pretended to be my secretary calling to inform them I mailed the wrong copy (I did not have a secretary). Since my submission was sent much earlier than the deadline, Tandy allowed me to resubmit as long as the revised copy was received prior to the deadline (and they agreed to discard the first one when it arrived).

I learned how to use spellcheck. I reprinted, repackaged, and mailed the application again.

This is an especially important lesson for future grant writers. Always leave yourself enough time before the deadline to step away from the grant and come back to it with fresh eyes and proofread and edit your writing. When you are too close to a project, it is hard to see the issues. If I had not submitted the application earlier, my career would have taken a vastly different turn.

I waited with bated breath for the Tandy grant award committee to review and decide. It felt like forever!

Then, the answer came.

"We won!"

I was ecstatic, and my principal was overjoyed. I was incredibly grateful to the grant writers and support staff at the district office. I have proudly kept a copy of my first grant to this day.

> Radio Shack
>
> Educational Grants Proposal
>
> Proposal Abstract
>
> We suggest that you complete this form AFTER writing the proposal body.
>
> INTRODUCTION: The Special Education Unit at our junior high school, consists of nine self contained classes of children who have been classified as emotionally handicapped, learning disabled or educable mentally retarded. We would like to develop a word processing written communication program utilizing Radio Shack Equipment that would meet the individual educational needs of these children.
>
> Our goal is to improve the students' written communication skills by using the TRS-80 Model 100 Portable Computer and the DWP-210 Letter Quality Printer as the motivational catalyst.
>
> NEEDS ASSESSMENT: PL94-142 the Federal Law, addresses the needs of the special education students. The law mandates that every student has the right to a free and appropriate public education in the least restrictive environment that will enable the child to develop to his or her own, maximum potential.
>
> The development of communication skills is a critical area in the development of the special education child to his or her own maximum potential. By enhancing the language arts curriculum through the utilization of the computer, the child who has previously had unrewarding writing experiences will demonstrate renewed interest and be more motivated to learn.
>
> OBJECTIVES: As a result of two periods a week of instructional activities utilizing twelve Radio Shack word processing systems for approximately twenty-four, seven through ninth grade special education students (two classes) at our junior high school during the period September 1984 through June 30, 1985, it is expected that participating students will demonstrate: statistically significant improvement (p<.05) over a matched control group in written communication skills as measured by pre-administration 1984 and post-administration 1985 of the State Education Department Writing Assessment Rating Scale; and demonstrate statistically significant improvement (p<.05) over a matched control group in word processing as measured by pre-administration September 1984 and post-administration June 1985 of a locally developed criterion reference test.
>
> ACTIVITIES: The two experimental classes and the control group will receive instruction in written communication skills according to each individual child's needs. In addition the two experimental classes (twenty-four special education students) will spend an average of 2 forty minute periods per week

FIGURE 2: MY FIRST GRANT WAS WRITTEN ON BANK STREET WRITER AND PRINTED ON A DOT MATRIX PRINTER.

This was the beginning of my grant writing career.

We won $15,000 worth of valuable computer equipment. That is equivalent to over $41,000 in purchasing power today. Imagine how significant it was for a first-time grant writer to win an award that large.

Each student got to use a TRS-8- Model 100 and I received cables, a heavy-duty dot-matrix printer, and a large Tandy Model 4.

I was able to teach not only my students word processing, but other students in the special education unit, as well.

They could print out their work, take it home and be proud of their accomplishments. Suddenly, nobody wanted to destroy their work anymore. My students could rework their writing and do it repeatedly, then we'd save printouts in accomplishment folders. They loved every minute of it.

Most importantly, I taught my students to enjoy schoolwork, writing and how to use computers.

I stayed in touch with Tandy and submitted my evaluation reports. All in all, we were incredibly happy with each other.

Next, the district office sent me an application for a matching Commodore 64 grant, and I won that grant, too. We won $9,000 and the school district matched that with another

$9,000. I outfitted my entire classroom with Commodore 64s and now I could also teach my students to use LOGO, a graphics art program, Bank Street Writer, and a spreadsheet program. Their writing and math skills were improving, and my special education classroom was leaping with learning.

My school had become an intermediate school grade 6 to 8 and a Magnet School. At that point, my school administrators started to look at me a little differently.

I was reassigned as a regular education Magnet School Teacher for Business Careers, Computers and Entrepreneurship. Special education students were mainstreamed into the computer room that I had already outfitted. With the new funding we also received IBM clone computers.

I was also part of the Magnet School curriculum writing initiative for teaching entrepreneurship and career education.

Beating the odds with curriculum.

It was September 1987, at the start of the school year, my Magnet School classes signed up to participate in the NY Newsday Stock Market Game. Each team of students received $100,000 in play money to develop a fictional portfolio and trade stocks. The team, along with their teacher, which achieved the highest portfolio value by the end of the semester would win a trip to Wall Street and participate in an award ceremony.

Since I was already involved in writing curriculum, I wrote a module for the stock market, teaching students how to use our computers to research a stock, chart it within a spreadsheet and anticipate what it might likely or possibly do.

I believe in doing things the right way. I did not allow my students to make trades without preliminary research and a basic understanding of the stock market.

When Black Monday happened, October 19, 1987, the day when the Dow Jones Industrial Average fell by 22% and marked the start of a global stock market decline, my students were flush with fictitious cash and had researched their picks. They were able to purchase stocks at exceptionally low prices.

And yes, we won the Stock Market Game and went to Wall Street. I have a beautiful plaque and another great memory.

Another life lesson learned. Research the data before you start anything because patience is a virtue in business.

Not getting the job.

With the achievement of my master's degree in special education and a postgraduate certificate in educational administration and supervision, I started taking certifying exams and I obtained all these licenses:

- ✓ School District Administrator/SAS

- ✓ Educational Administrator - Funded Programs Management Instruction Specialist Levels I, II

- ✓ Educational Administrator - Funded Programs Management Instruction Specialist Levels III, IV

- ✓ Assistant Principal (Administration) in Day High Schools

- ✓ Assistant Principal of Day Elementary, Intermediate and Junior High Schools

- ✓ Assistant Administrative Director

- ✓ Supervisor of Special Education Program

- ✓ Educational Administrator-Senior Educational Research

- ✓ Evaluation & Program Planning Instruction Specialist - Levels III, IV

My professor at Brooklyn College emphasized the close connection between educational policy and politics. As part of our coursework, he encouraged us to actively engage with local political clubs to gain firsthand experience. Additionally, he assigned us the task of writing articles about these events and submitting them to local newspapers for publication.

I participated in local political activities and attended many local community events. I networked and made friends in high places. I was applying to every high-level position opening within the DOE. Mostly I made it to the last round of interviews. On the quiet, many hints and promises were made to me. And yet, I had a folder, plump with rejection letters.

Educational admin: grant writer at the district office.

In 1990, to my surprise, someone placed a job posting in my teacher's mailbox with the handwritten words: "Please Apply!"

The job was for an Interim Acting Educational Administrator at the district office (DO), in the grant writing office. Although this was the culmination of all my work, I initially thought it was a prank. There was one more round of interviews and finally, I was hired. Imagine my private joy.

Phyllis Gonon, the Deputy Superintendent hired me, even though at my interview I did not know the definition of the acronym RFP (request for proposals). She hired me based on my achievements.

The grant writing office consisted of my mentor Phyllis, three experienced grant writers, Heidi, Billie, and I am at a loss for the name of the third grant writer, the district office accountant, and three secretaries.

I was the newbie in the grant writing office and Phyllis Gonon was the toughest no-nonsense boss I have ever known. I am forever grateful to her for her mentorship and for bringing out my absolute best and much more.

I did not require a secretary, as I was already exclusively writing using WordPerfect, and teaching students to write creatively on a computer. My colleagues knew the cost for rent, telephone, or a part time teacher, etc. and I knew how to input the equations. I was able to create budgets with equations on spreadsheets because I had already taught this to my students for stock research. When I modified something in my budgets, the spreadsheet automatically recalculated.

I proved myself again when I shared my budget templates or assisted my colleagues with their budgets. Everyone was still using adding machines with paper rolls, pencils, and erasers to calculate in 1990. I was amazed how fast their fingers were as we discussed a project. I can still hear the adding machine in my head when I think back to those days.

The district office accountant was my go-to resource for understanding costs for the development of federal budgets, administrative costs, projected salaries, and expenses. I later transitioned to Microsoft Word and Excel.

I worked in the grant office at the DO (Community School District), for two years, winning more than $11 million in grants for creative programs that would match the needs of the schools, with the mission of the funding source.

I was finding new ways to engage children in reading and in math through the arts. In addition, I was engaging parents in parenting programs, helping with family mental health and counseling services, and providing teachers and staff with professional development.

At the DO, I was writing grants for seventeen schools (12 elementary and 5 intermediate). These grants were funded for multiple years and then later my replacement grant writers at the DO reapplied, using, and updating my initial grants.

A sampling of the grants I wrote and won, at the DO.
This is a just a partial, nostalgic list that I have kept among my keepsakes over the years.

- ✓ Drug Free Schools Federal Activities Grant ($351,756)
- ✓ Drug Free Schools and Communities ($200,000)
- ✓ HHS Youth Gang Drug Prevention Program ($210,000)
- ✓ Family Systems Theory, Drug Free Schools ($293,771)
- ✓ Alternative Family Education, Drug Free Schools ($380,028)
- ✓ HHS Youth Gang Drug Prevention ($150,000)
- ✓ Title VII Special Populations ($180,000)
- ✓ Title VII Transitional Programs ($174,681)
- ✓ Title VII Family English Literacy ($172,657)
- ✓ Targeted Primary Prevention Demonstration, OSAP ($139,660)
- ✓ ISS LEP (9) School Year Grants, NYS ($152,000)
- ✓ ISS LEP (10) Summer School Grants, NYS ($142,000)
- ✓ Parenting Education Program, NYS ($68,000)
- ✓ Targeted Primary Prevention, OSAP ($144,122)
- ✓ Fund for Innovation, NYS ($50,000)
- ✓ Multicultural Education, NYC ($30,000)

The youth gang grant.

My most memorable grant was the HHS Youth Gang Prevention Grant.

As the office newbie, I would get a new Federal Register on my desk every day and a few at once on some days with the incoming mail. (Today, everything is online. However, then, everything was hardcopy.)

Sometimes the Federal Register was a quarter of an inch thick and other times as large as two inches, bound. I would also receive all the periodicals listing currently available grants.

My daily routine was to weed through all these and then read the RFPs that held the promise of our eligibility.

I would write a synopsis of viable grants for the local schools and the school district for the team meeting and pitch the grants that I thought we should apply for. Next, the Deputy Superintendent would ask about our current projects and assign and schedule our workload; then it was back to our desks. Our office was always busy.

When I found the *HHS Youth Gang Prevention Grant* in the Federal Register, I was super excited. I knew in my heart of hearts we had a youth gang problem in our community and that this grant was what we needed.

I ran (not walked) to my supervisor's office to tell her the news. Her answer, "There are no youth gangs in our district!"

Of course, I knew she was wrong. I had been in the classroom; I taught in an intermediate school and overheard many things. There were whispers about a baseball bat drive-by and other group acts of violence.

After badgering Phyllis, the answer I next received was, "Libby, if you can prove there are youth gangs in our school district, you can write the grant."

Writing this grant was to be a real challenge, I was stepping out of my personal comfort zone. I was raised in a very sheltered environment, attending parochial school until I entered college.

My younger brother was an NYPD police officer (quite possibly a sergeant at that time), and I naively thought the police would be happy to help me. I called the local precinct looking for information and I was stonewalled. I reached out to the youth officer at the precinct, and again the answer was that there are no youth gangs.

And then one day, I was told I had a visitor at the DO. She was in plain clothes, and she introduced herself with, "I wasn't here, and you do not know me." The woman handed me a white envelope filled with everything you always wanted to know about local youth gangs. And then she was gone. I recognized her voice from the calls I made, but as requested, I forgot her name.

She also gave me the name of an individual and suggested I try to locate them. He was the head of a roundtable of youth gangs.

I found him. I met with him. It was all very clandestine.

However, when I wrote the grant I certainly had more anecdotal information than most. The program I developed for the grant proposal would outreach to the community's at-risk youth. Everything was planned with the goal of getting kids off the streets and into a meaningful school experience. We would entice students to attend school with participation in very specialized after school programs – one of which included the use of a recording music studio and other artistic offerings, like comic book arts.

After identifying the needs and interests that would get area youths to reenter a school and become engaged in a positive activity, I built the costs into the budget. The reading and math program and other subjects would be taught with material relevant to their interests.

We made sure to include mental health support systems, and parent and family engagement as well. As a result, many attendance officers joined my cause.

To my recollection, a total of four Youth Gang Prevention Grants were awarded that year by Health and Human Services (HHS) and we were one of them. We were awarded $360,000 and it was funded for a few additional years, as well.

Life was stressful.

I was working 9 to 5 outside the home, a departure from my 8 to 3 schedule. My children were now in their formative years, and I was working longer hours than I did as a teacher. I was bringing more work home, staying up late in the evenings, and working from home on weekends.

There were more and more grants to write and just not enough hours in the day. During that time, I won many grants for the DO that were funded for multiple years.

I began to feel like the cash register that kept on giving for the DO. The stress level of working on multiple competitive grant applications simultaneously was unbelievable.

Most days I worked through lunch because I was so passionate about the programs I was developing. My creativity and determination knew no bounds. I was often so engrossed in my work that I would be surprised when the lights were turned off and people were saying, "Have a nice evening."

I kept writing and writing and winning. My colleagues were also winning. We were perhaps the school district winning the most grants in the city at that time because Community School District 18 invested in a grant writing office and it paid off, big time.

Again, I was still a newbie and the other grant writers had many more years of experience than me. It did not make me popular with my colleagues, when my supervisor would say things like, "Touch Libby, she has the Midas touch!"

I was and am incredibly grateful for the absolute best on-the-job training and mentoring. I had come so far and achieved so much.

However, after two years, the stress of the job took its toll and I asked to return to the classroom.

I had heard friends and colleagues say the phrase "Touch Libby..." so often that when on vacation in 1992 in Las Vegas, I saw a slot machine called *The Midas Touch*, I thought it was some great sign from heaven.

Maybe it was and maybe it wasn't, but I put in a few quarters. I won $300! That's about $700 equivalent, today. I considered it my tip for my hard work at the DO.

When I began teaching again, I had to get some papers signed and returned to the DO during my lunch hour. Guess what I found out? They had hired three new grant writers to replace me after I left. What's more, they were using the text of my original grants to write new ones. Boilerplate pieces for organizational capacity, history, and fiscal management, among other parts that could be tweaked. They were also being used for new grant applications from the same schools.

Three grant writers came to the front desk to greet me when they heard I was in the building. They wanted to meet the woman whose grants on which they were working. I felt so validated after our brief conversation, and I left feeling quite accomplished.

Opening my own grant writing business.

I had learned so much at the DO. I returned to my school and went back into the classroom. My colleagues and principal were happy to have me back. And I was happy to be back. The familiar faces, the familiar backdrop, and reduced hours were just what I needed. Teaching 8 to 3 gave me the time to open my own grant writing business, after school and on weekends.

I started a fax newsletter called NYCGrantsWatch. My clients wanted to know what grants were available. I authored weekly articles about what was trending in the grant world and sent a weekly global fax to 300 subscribers.

My middle daughter Lani helped compile the grants to add to the newsletter and proofread my grant applications. Today Lani is the very efficient and well-organized manager of all grant researchers, editors, and proofreaders for our grant listings.

I had an eye injury early on in a pregnancy, and for a while I was not allowed to drive long distances. My teaching assignment was then changed to less than a 5-minute drive from home. I was transferred to PS 29 in Staten Island, an elementary school where I taught third and fourth grade. This became another lesson on how an exceedingly tricky situation can become an opportunity.

This new life change made my life easier. I had less driving, I was teaching younger students, and I had about two more hours in my day to devote to my family and my grant writing business. I was also saving a lot of money on travel expenses.

Writing curriculum.

My skill set continued to grow. The combination of grant writing and teaching combined makes you an excellent researcher of best practices and a well thought out curriculum writer. I could evaluate the needs of my students and set long-term and short-term goals. And, of course, I developed objectives and activities to achieve those goals. I had an exceptional understanding of the need for evaluation, pre- and post-testing, and parental engagement.

My then School Principal, Linda Manfredi, and my Assistant Principal Annmarie Vallebuona, at PS 29 provided me with many opportunities to use my skills. I wrote both a literacy grant and a beautification grant for the school. As a classroom teacher, I was part of the school team that wrote America's Choice Literacy Curricula.

The NYC Department of Education hired me to work after school, on the Elementary School, Balanced Literacy Curriculum, and the Social Studies Curriculum.

A client from my grant writing business hired me to Co-author the GEPC: Global Education Preschool Curriculum, which was an anti-bullying curriculum that required a lot of research into best practices. It took a long time to get the format right, like authoring this book, but after that it was smooth sailing.

Running for city council.

While living and teaching on Staten Island, it became apparent that political change was needed. I had all my experience in Brooklyn when attending political functions under my administration coursework.

A seat became vacant, and I ran for NYC City Council in a special election for the 50th councilmanic district. I did not win but I learned a lot and gained insight into issues and the changes needed. I debated on live TV, gave press conferences, and wrote policy papers daily. Eugene (Gene) Lerman, my campaign treasurer and a good family friend was indispensable. He made sure we maxed out on the NYC four to one match for campaign contributions and filed everything properly. I really believe that my political campaigns prepared me to write web copy for GrantWatch.

I was a very hands-on candidate. A micromanager, some might say. That kind of dedication and attention to detail can sometimes drive peers and staff crazy. However, with me, there are so many rough drafts of everything I do. I keep writing until my gut says, "It is a go!"

I love input and always welcome feedback. But, if my name is on it, then all content must reflect who I am.

FIGURE 3: ONE OF THE FLYERS FROM THE SPECIAL ELECTION.

I ran again two years later in the primary and general election. The political parties and climate of today are not at all representative of 2001. Or maybe I was just young and naïve.

FIGURE 4: MAGNETS THAT WE DISTRIBUTED FOR THE PRIMARY AND GENERAL ELECTION OF 2001.

I was endorsed by the *New York Times* and many other local news organizations. Today, I am not quite certain they would endorse me as my views have evolved significantly as I have matured. Anyway, I am not running again, and I no longer live in New York State.

I'm too busy anyway. I have a business to run. *GrantWatch* helps more people in one day, in a fair and equitable manner, than I could ever achieve as a local political figure in today's environment.

More about GrantWatch later, but it is safe to say that my website has brought more opportunities and leveled the playing field for small and large nonprofits, businesses, and individuals.

Everything we do builds upon some previous life experience. Nothing is ever a waste.

Primary Day, 9/11 Attack on World Trade Center.

It was early morning, September 11, 2001, Primary Day in New York. The last day for GOTV, to get out the vote.

David Beryl Phillips, my campaign manager, sent Erin Cohan, a campaign staffer and me to a small part of Brooklyn, for GOTV (get out the vote). This was a section of the 50th

Councilmanic District that extended from Staten Island into another borough.

That primary morning, while standing the required feet from a voting location to greet future constituents, a police officer pulled up. He told us that we had to take cover. A plane had hit one of the Twin Towers and we might be at war.

I needed to get home to my children! I remember telling Erin to make a full stop at red lights, look both ways and proceed cautiously. I also promised to pay for any tickets she might get. We were petrified. We made it back over the Verrazano Bridge to Staten Island, a minute before they closed the bridge.

I went home to kiss and hug my family, and then went to my Staten Island school to be of help. Not all parents would be coming to pick up their children. You could see the plumes of smoke from Staten Island. I do not know where my campaign staff slept that night. It was a crazy time.

All political campaigns were at a hard stop. My staff, as well as everyone else, wanted to help in some way. The news was horrific. We all wanted to give blood, but it wasn't needed.

Adrenaline was running high in my office. Erin, Lynda, and Antoinette called restaurants, drug stores, and anyone who was answering their phones, and loaded up six vans filled with hot food, fruit, snacks, drinks, and medical supplies. And then, together with Jimmy Max, a local restaurateur, and his restaurant staff, we all went over on the Staten Island Ferry.

My team of first responders.

It was my team and the National Guard on the ferry.

The ferry captain sent his first mate down with a message that he wanted me to come up to the wheelhouse. He wanted to honor what we were doing and have me drive the ferry.

"I drove the Ferry, but I didn't park it," I would tell my friends years later when there was a ferry collision, in the news. I just held the wheel straight, had a conversation with the captain and someone took pictures.

We arrived in Manhattan and every vehicle and street in the area looked like it was covered with a very thick coat of sand (like after a sandstorm), but it was ash. While my staff walked the perimeter, I coordinated with fire captains to discuss where we should set up our tables, with the supplies we brought.

Everyone was beside themselves with grief and all I kept hearing were the miscommunications that happened when first responders came on the scene. These grown men who could easily carry one hundred pounds of equipment were openly crying because they had warned the city about the need for a unified radio frequency. And now it was too late.

When my staff finally came back to the vans, they too were crying. Some were sick having been confronted by human remains in the ash. I was grateful that I did not go with them and that I was busy getting instructions for my team.

We were directed to the bottom of what I call the bucket brigade. There were teams set up to sift through the rubble and pass it down the line to the next responder.

We set up folding tables and started feeding first responders and we also provided medical supplies for cuts and bruises that we had brought with us for minor injuries.

FIGURE 5: ONE OF THE FIREFIGHTERS, SO GRATEFUL FOR THE FOOD MY TEAM BROUGHT, TOOK A FEW PICTURES OF MY TEAM, AND HANDED ME THE DISK FROM HIS CAMERA.

In the above image you can see me offering a smile, an apple, and a cup of water to one of the individuals tirelessly sifting through the debris to find those who were lost. It was a small gesture, but necessary to show their efforts were not lost on the rest of us.

A siren would blast like in a movie about coal miners when a part of the building was unsteady or started to fall. The adrenaline rush took over. I felt immortal.

I gave no thought as to how what I was breathing might affect my health later.

The siren blasted three times that day. Thank the heavens for the people who each time just grabbed our hands and helped us run for safety.

It was late that night when we ran out of food. My staff had dished out a mountain of food to some very weary first responders. I had spent the day offering as much empathy as I had in me, and then some, to everyone who needed to talk or just cry.

My three angels.

My three-campaign staff members: Lynda Forlenza, Antoinette and Erin Cohan greeted me one morning when I walked up the steps to my campaign office, wearing white shirts with *Libby's Angels* written in red script.

That was so unbelievable, I started to cry and then they ushered me out because we had so much more to do.

That same day, we brought hot meals and fresh fruit for the first responders to the staging area. However, by then, President George W. Bush was visiting Ground Zero, so we had to set up a short distance away. When we left Manhattan, more food and supplies were being dropped off at the campaign office. That night we went to the Fresh Kills Landfill on Staten Island, where the ash was being brought to be sifted through for human remains and evidence.

As we went up with our vans of food and medical supplies for first responders, we were flagged down by a police officer and told that the family of a man named Ken White had delivered a cake. It was his birthday, and he did not make it out of the Towers. They wanted candles to be lit and *Happy Birthday* to be sung for him at Fresh Kills, where they believed his remains might be.

We did just that for Ken, and we contacted the Staten Island Advance, the borough newspaper to write the story, so the family would know that we honored their wishes. Below is only a portion of the article. My apologies that the bottom half of the article went missing over the years.

SDAY, SEPTEMBER 25, 2001   A 3

Recovery workers make a wish for missing Island man

- **Officials at landfill sing for Islander who would have celebrated his 51st birthday yesterday**

By CHAN-JOO MOON
ADVANCE STAFF WRITER

His name was Ken. He would have turned 51 yesterday.

That's all that several dozen workers at the Fresh Kills landfill knew about a man who is listed as missing in the World Trade Center tragedy. Yet they celebrated his birthday last night.

A man who said he was Ken's brother brought a birthday cake to Sanitation Police Officer Carlos Rodriguez, who was stationed at the security check point at Muldoon Avenue. He asked Rodriguez to take the cake to the men sifting through the tons of debris coming from Ground Zero.

Sanitation officers later gave the cake to Mid-Island City Council candidate Libby Hikind, who arrived at the landfill to deliver donated food to the workers.

Ms. Hikind said she brought the cake to the food tent, where about 25 workers gathered around it.

"We all took a sigh after I relayed the message. They just said, 'OK guys. Let's do it,'" she said.

They lit the two candles of the numbers 5 and 1, and sang "Happy Birthday" to Ken, she

White

partake because of her kosher diet, saved the plastic "Happy Birthday" sign and the two candles to give to the family, should they contact her.

The workers sifting through the debris at the landfill include police detectives, FBI agents, Secret Service agents, Bureau of Alcohol, Tobacco and Firearms officers, National Guardsmen and some retired cops.

Advance records showed that Kenneth White of Richmond Valley would have celebrated his 51st birthday yesterday. Contacted at home, his wife, Catherine, said her husband's brother, Thomas White, came from New Jersey last night to visit the house. Although he did not mention the cake, she theorized that he stopped at the landfill before the visit. Thomas White could not be reached last night.

Kenneth White worked in the telephone division of Cantor Fitzgerald, on the 105th floor of Tower 1. He was a member of Local 3 of the International Brotherhood of Electrical Workers.

He last called home on the morning of Sept. 11 and spoke to his oldest son, Brian, 23.

"He said 'What was it that hit?' My son said, 'A plane.' He said it felt like a bomb and he fell down, but he was OK," she said. "He said people were grabbing masks and running and he

Yacht Club. He had a lively sense of humor and enjoyed helping neighbors with tasks such as pruning trees.

A native of Brooklyn, he was brought to Tottenville as a child. He was a graduate of Tottenville High School.

Mr. White served in the Air Force from 1969 to 1972 as a carpenter. Part of his service was in Germany, where he met his wife, who was a civilian employee serving as a secretary in the Air Force.

They married and lived for a year and a half in Ireland before coming to Great Kills in the mid-1970s. They moved to Tottenville in the late 1970s and settled in Richmond Valley in 1989.

The family still holds out hope that Mr. White is alive.

"It's very rough. [We're] still trying to comprehend, still trying to believe what happened," Mrs. White said.

Ms. Hikind said her office has been regularly bringing donations of hot food to the dump to supplement the food that is provided by the Red Cross. Last night, she purchased the food with her own funds because she ran out of restaurants to call, she said.

Ms. Hikind said the landfill workers are "helping families achieve closure."

Businesses that donated food to her effort include:

Afternoone's Meats; A&S Pork Store; Mike's Place; the Staaten; Nuccio; Jimmy Max; Parsonage; Iguana Cafe;

FIGURE 6: STATEN ISLAND ADVANCE 9/25/2001

Two weeks later I won the Primary election. But alas, in the end, I did not win the General election. I walked away from politics having received a respectable 35% of the vote.

After the general election in November, I had a lot of free time on my hands, because I had taken a leave of absence to run for office. I could not return to my teaching assignment until the beginning of the following school year.

Child Health Plus: The grant that kept on giving.

It's a little fuzzy, since it has been 22+ years, but I believe I wrote the Child Health Plus grant during this period.

The Child Health Plus grant obtained free and sliding scale health insurance for children on Staten Island. Healthy children make a world of difference for generations to come.

I had formed a coalition of every nonprofit that felt they could outreach to underserved and uninsured children. We had an extraordinarily long and full conference table. This grant was funded for $700,000 in the first year and was renewed for many years afterwards.

The last time I called the JCC of Staten Island to inquire, in 2014, I was told that over 50,000 children had been signed up to receive health insurance. During a leave of absence for one year, I became the grant writer for Audrey Cohen College which later became Metropolitan College of New York. I worked on a federal ETA Career Training Grant for them, which I won. I had to fly in an airplane for the first time since 9/11, in May 2002, to a conference in Florida. Having witnessed the devastation at Ground Zero, I never thought I would fly again. And yet, here I was taking another step into the unknown to see where it would lead.

Project Liberty hired me, after 9/11.

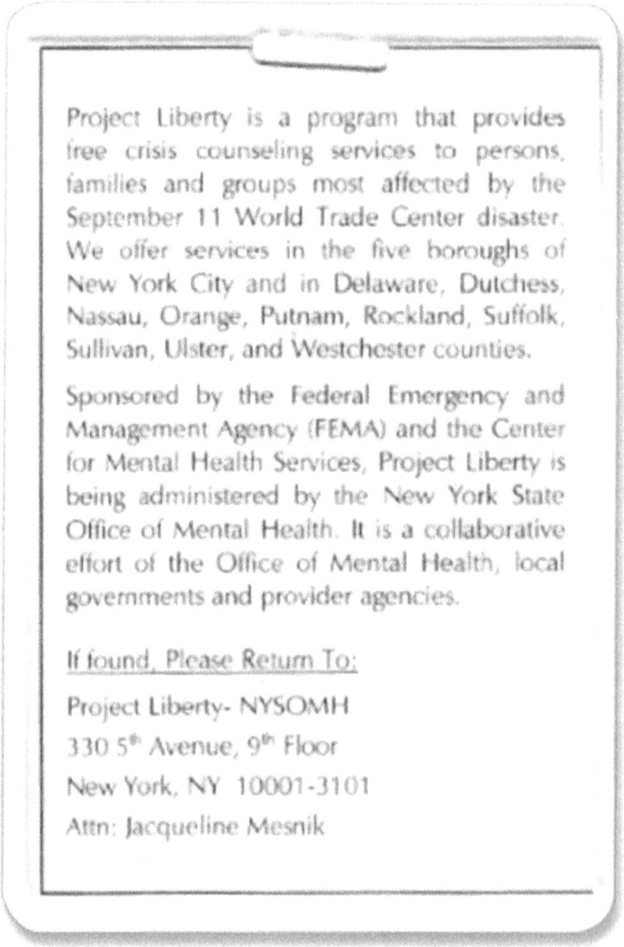

Project Liberty is a program that provides free crisis counseling services to persons, families and groups most affected by the September 11 World Trade Center disaster. We offer services in the five boroughs of New York City and in Delaware, Dutchess, Nassau, Orange, Putnam, Rockland, Suffolk, Sullivan, Ulster, and Westchester counties.

Sponsored by the Federal Emergency and Management Agency (FEMA) and the Center for Mental Health Services, Project Liberty is being administered by the New York State Office of Mental Health. It is a collaborative effort of the Office of Mental Health, local governments and provider agencies.

If found, Please Return To:
Project Liberty- NYSOMH
330 5th Avenue, 9th Floor
New York, NY 10001-3101
Attn: Jacqueline Mesnik

FIGURE 7: PROJECT LIBERTY IS A PROGRAM THAT PROVIDES FREE CRISIS COUNSELING SERVICES TO PERSONS, FAMILIES, AND GROUPS MOST AFFECTED BY THE SEPTEMBER 11TH WORLD TRADE CENTER DISASTER.

I became a Project Liberty Crisis Intervention Counselor and I managed and trained a team of ten counselors I was meeting people in college cafeterias, speaking in libraries and fire stations, making fast evaluations for needed services, and providing referral phone numbers and resources. Most of my speaking engagements were impromptu to avoid red tape and were well received. I would stay afterwards and ask my teammates to be available one on one for anyone who needed to talk to someone.

My team would call me at odd hours looking for appropriate providers for referrals, suggestions on where to outreach and questions of how to respond. We continued to add to our local provider lists for referral suggestions. We had crisis counselor team meetings in my home and in libraries. My teammates submitted their notes of interactions. I did all the team paperwork and submitted it to payroll.

However, my true mission as an intervention counselor was to be the most empathetic person I could be, listening to anyone that needed to speak. I was so busy!

I remember facilitating a Project Liberty group conversation at a firehouse in Staten Island with one of my team members. There were many firefighters at the dinner table. The alarm went off and I blinked-- everyone was gone! We walked around the empty firehouse garage and saw everyone's shoes, on either side of where moments ago the fire engines had been.

My team was dedicated enough that we waited until they returned and continued. After the firehouse incident, FDNY contacted me and wanted my team to work directly with them. Unfortunately, it was not meant to be. There was too much red tape, new certifications needed that would take too long, so we continued with Project Liberty.

I returned to teaching when the school year started. My grant writing business was in full swing when I returned to teaching 3rd and 4th grade balanced literacy. I also wrote and won more grants for my school. I wrote a grant that beautified the school hallway, with students' designing ceramic tiles that were then baked and hung.

In addition, I wrote another grant for the school district to add Holocaust books, categorized by appropriate age levels to school libraries.

Over a period of two years, together with my daughter Lani, we wrote and won ten Homeland Security Grants for my faith-based nonprofit clients.

Over the next couple of years, I wrote five winning Early Learn Grants, and another five Universal PreK grants. I won Alzheimer's funding, grants for parenting, and a resource center grant, Parent to Parent for parents of children with disabilities. I also wrote a plan for a diagnostic and treatment center for special needs children and their families (which was later sold to a hospital), and many other grants.

I believe I have raised billions of dollars through my own grant writing because the Early Learn grants alone were renewed repeatedly and each was well over a million dollars per year.

Many of the grants I have written were renewed multiple times.

I retired from teaching and found my artsy side.

I finally retired in July 2009, from the NYC Department of Education with almost 29 years at the Department, and many years of teaching in private preschool, elementary, and Sunday school. Teaching was a lifelong career that, as I explained earlier, started at the age of fifteen after school and on Sundays.

FIGURE 8: GRANT FOR HOLOCAUST BOOKS.

I decided to take a real break and enrolled in oil painting and stained-glass classes and set out to re-explore my inner creative senses. I also continued to write grants for my clients.

But art was my time to rest and rejuvenate from all the years of punching a clock.

As my children now say, "Yeah, mom, your retirement only lasted about six months!"

They are right because while doing artwork, my business head was spinning. I already knew what I could do with a website because I had a background in computers. It did not take me long to realize I needed to get back to being relevant and contributing. I needed to do something to refocus.

My clients wanted to know what grants were available. Their pain point was that by the time periodicals told them about available grants, the deadlines were too close. They expected me to solve the problem.

More than anyone, I understood the need.

My clients needed funding, but most could not afford to hire a grant researcher. They also could not reconcile spending hours researching grants.

As for myself, I kept falling into the rabbit hole of searching for grants for my own clients. I understood how frustrating it can be when you search for grants only to find they are expired or have not been offered this year at all.

Searching for grants using the traditional method in those days was very time consuming. You would go to the Foundation Library in Manhattan and spend hours and hours looking at foundations, trying to see if they might fund your mission. It was frustrating and often unsuccessful. After all your hours of research, you might either miss the deadline or find that they weren't offering a grant that year.

I was thinking back to when I started out in the District Office. I would get a pile of the Federal Register books and every other grant newsletter dropped on my desk, on Monday morning. It was my job as the newbie to go through them all and write up briefs of grants I thought were possibilities for our team meetings.

Most school districts did not even have my position, and some did not even have one grant writer.

Nonprofits had the same issue unless they were a major national nonprofit. My client base was growing, but I wanted to level the playing field and let everybody know what funding opportunities were currently available.

And that's basically how it all came about.

The start of GrantWatch.

I knew I was onto something. My goal was to offer a one stop place where everybody could go, and find currently available federal, state, local, corporate, and foundation grants.

I started building the web version of my faxed newsletter in December 2009, *NYCGrantsWatch*.

While I couldn't code in PHP, or set up a database, I knew that what I wanted was to create a grants website that would be updated daily and more current than the weekly faxed newsletter I had published years ago.

I worked on the first draft of my home page on my best friend's kitchen table in Florida. Ghita lived in the same community as my parents. Since retiring from teaching, I was able to visit more often.

Ghita had absolutely no grant writing background and that was a good thing for me, because I could read text aloud to her while she prepared dinner and hear and see her response. If it didn't make sense to Ghita or wasn't clear, I would modify the web content.

What I knew in my sleep was confusing to others, so my goal was to demystify grants and level the playing field for large and small organizations. I bounced my ideas off my parents as well. They had both been teachers and had each owned a business.

My daughter Lani had recently written some Homeland Security grant applications with me. She was also helping me find grant content for the website.

I started building the website with a student who had just finished his coursework in PHP, a programming language, and MySQL database training. GrantWatch was basically his paid internship to put into practice what he learned in class. We both learned a lot working together. He went on to have a family and has worked on some interesting projects as a private and government security contractor.

Subsequently, as we grew and expanded, we found out that some of our code was called spaghetti strings by more experienced developers. Over the years we rewrote and redesigned – but thankfully it all worked initially, and we were able to provide a wonderful experience for the grant seeker.

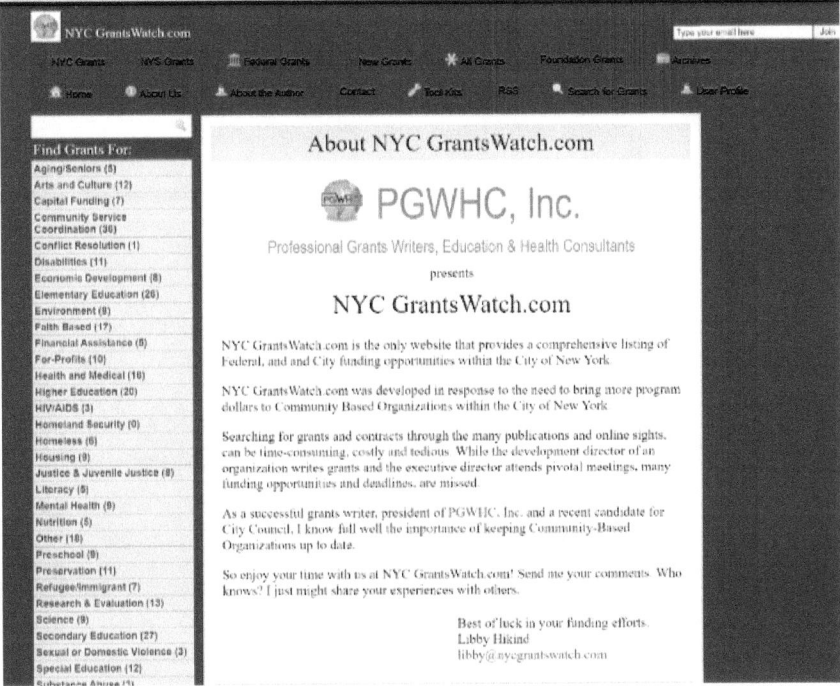

FIGURE 9: FEBRUARY 2010 NYCGRANTSWATCH.COM

You will notice in all these images how the website has transformed over the years.

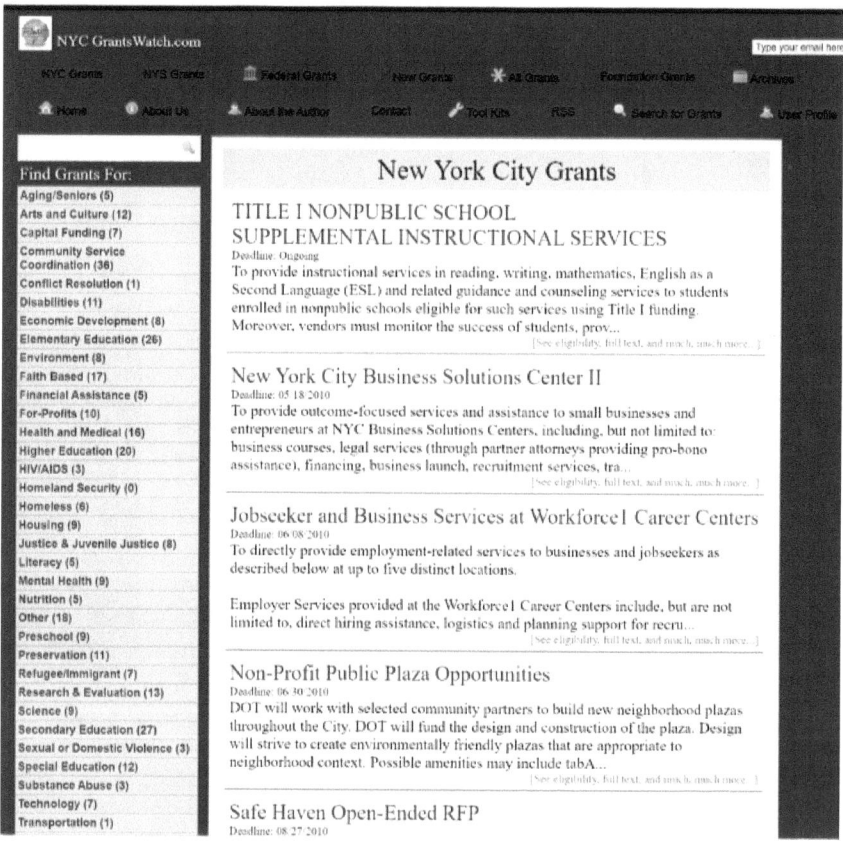

FIGURE 10: THE WEBSITE WAS FINALLY READY TO GO ONLINE.

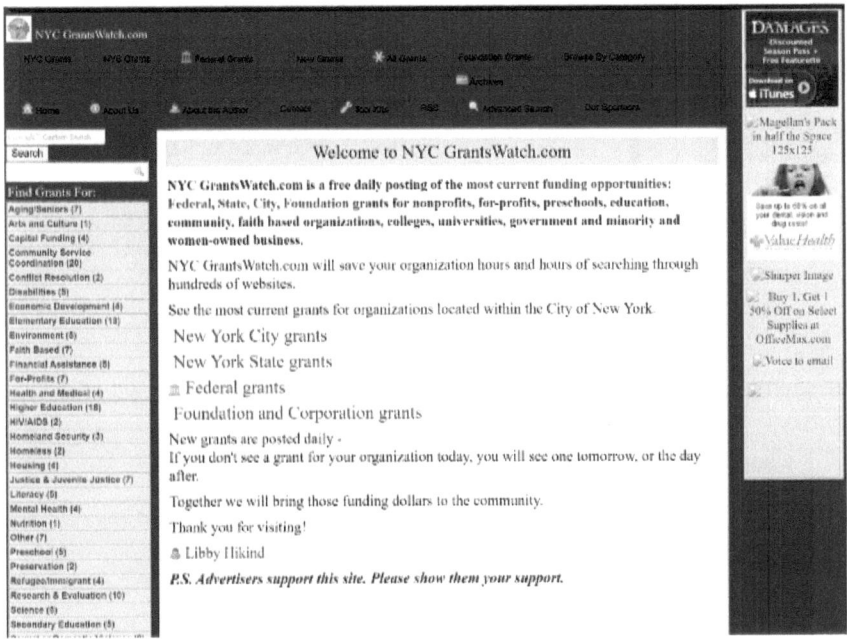

FIGURE 11: WE ADDED NEW YORK STATE GRANTS.

We learned the hard way that a free comprehensive website, supported only by PPC (pay for click ads), was not going to work. We also learned that giving 24 hours of free access meant that no one would pay to subscribe. People would come and go with 24-hour access.

I felt a bit defeated, but I had the ability to be patient because I was retired from a government job and still had all my grant writing clients.

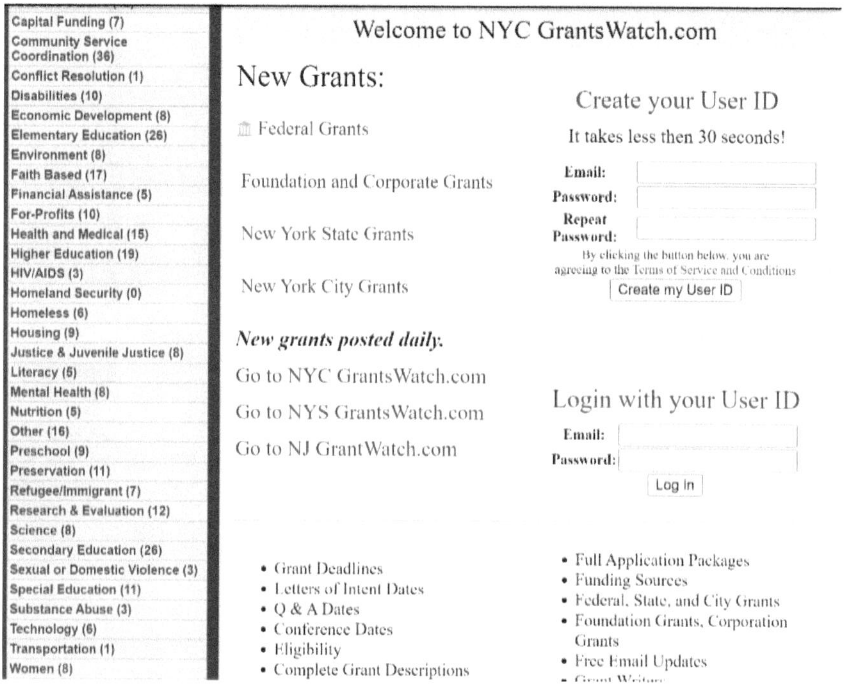

FIGURE 12: WE ADDED NEW JERSEY GRANTS.

Finally, we made our first dollar in May 2010, from a subscriber, after there was no longer free access. People, it seemed, were willing to pay for our service of currently available grants, reviewing the grants, and the grant details in our proprietary format.

FIGURE 13: AUGUST 2010 WE ADDED NJ GRANTS.

We added grant categories and combined others. We added new grants daily and with the push of a button archived all past due grants.

Reviewing grants for the federal government.

At this same time, I was also a remote field reader/peer reviewer of grants. I was asked to go to Washington, D.C. in 2011 and review grants at the Omni Hotel with other peer reviewers. Our task was to identify strengths and weaknesses in each section of the ten grant applications assigned to our team.

For me, seeing the full review process first-hand was eye opening. You realize what makes the reader confident and what makes them wary of the nonprofit's proposed program.

They removed the beds from the assigned hotel rooms. With three readers and a supervisor in each room, each reviewer in the same room read the same ten applications. The applications were scored according to a checklist of items that needed to be included in the response and discussed over a period of a few days. When our scores for any section of an application were too far apart, we would discuss until some kind of compromise with the supervisor was reached.

When we finished, they gave us more!

There were 1,000 grants read in those few days at the Omni and only forty with the highest scores were funded. If you have ever written a federal grant, then you know it takes over the entire organization. A federal grant can take a minimum of four to six weeks of work.

We expanded the reach of the website.

Meeting so many people in the grant industry and having taken calls from all over the United States from grant writers looking for grants, it was time to add locations.

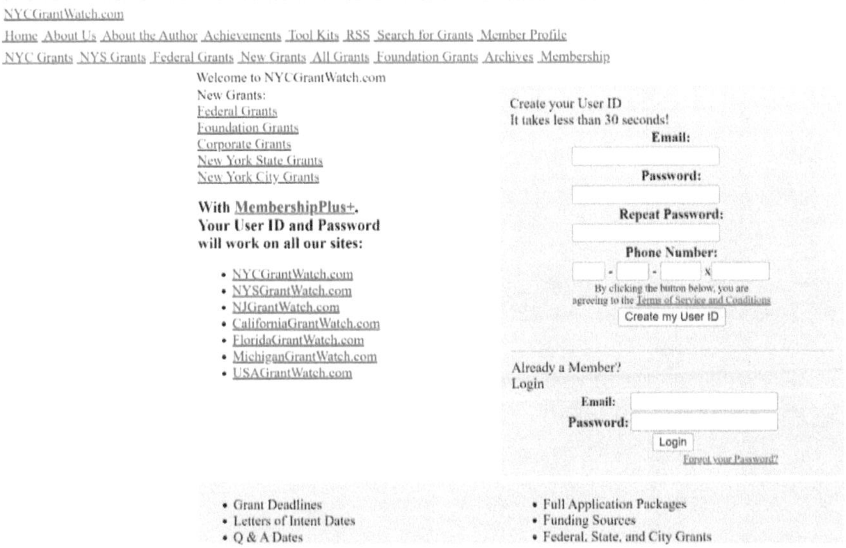

FIGURE 14: AUGUST 2011 YOU CAN SEE US EXPERIMENTING WITH ADDING VARIOUS STATES.

Little by little, we expanded to NY State, and then New Jersey, and we tried adding a few major states.

The start of GrantWatch.com

Our name changed from NYCGrantsWatch to GrantWatch.com and our logo changed a few times over the years. Today we are happily branded.

We created subdomains for each state and never lost sight of NYC, keeping it as its own subdomain as well. Each state as a subdomain, was created, for example like this: Florida.GrantWatch.com, NewYork.GrantWatch.com

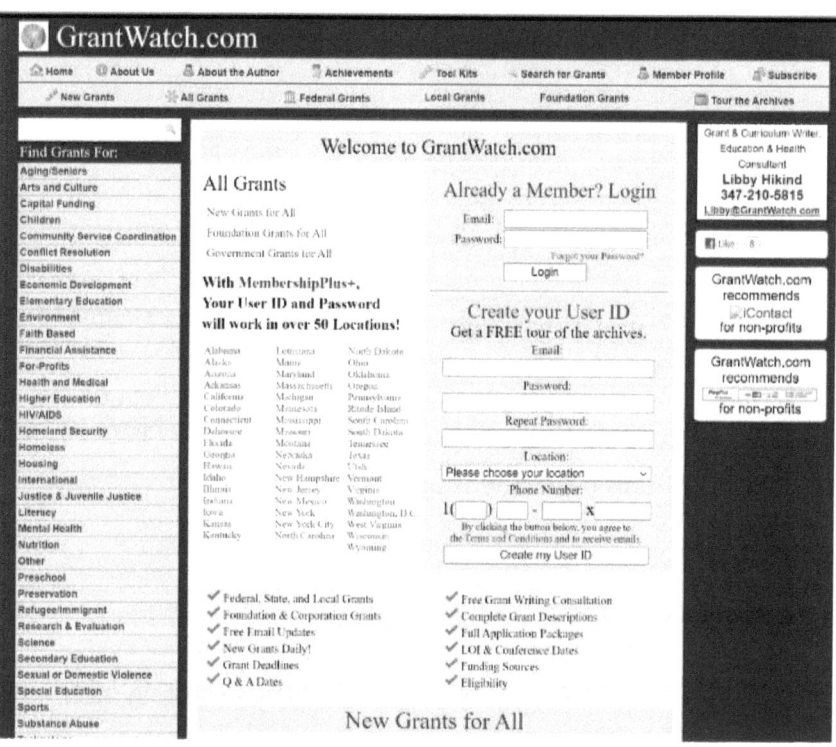

FIGURE 15: 2012 WE ADDED ALL THE USA STATES AS SUBDOMAINS.

FIGURE 16: IN 2015 THE WEBSITE HAD A FRESH LOOK AND 1,703 GRANTS. AFTER THE STATES, WE ADDED THE USA COMPACT FREE ASSOCIATIONS, USA TERRITORIES, CANADA, ISRAEL AND INTERNATIONAL.

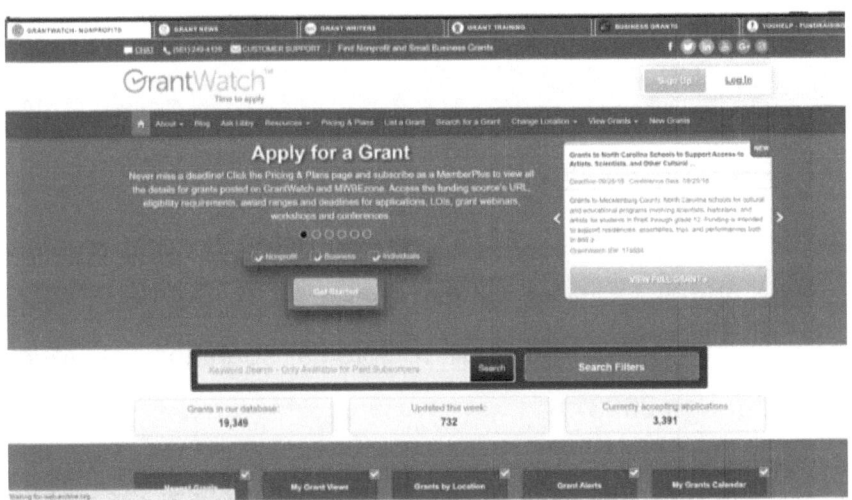

FIGURE 17: THE 2018 BRAND-NEW LOOK, NEW LOGO AND 3,391 GRANTS AVAILABLE.

By September of 2022, we were already maintaining 7,000 to 8,000 currently available grants with fresh blog content on the GrantNews blog, daily.

To appreciate these numbers, understand that there are ongoing grants that have no due dates, but when the money runs out, they will close, and most grants have deadlines for when the application process ends. To maintain the numbers of currently available grants we need to add about 700 to 1,000 new grants per week.

FIGURE 18: DECEMBER 25, 2023

As of December 25th, 2023, we had uploaded and created graphs and illustrations for more than 3,138,356 Form 990s from grant funders and grant recipients, spanning the years 2015 through 2023.

The 990s are government tax forms that provide the public with information about nonprofits. Of these, we had information from 276,489 grant funders and 630,067 grant recipients. We added a 990-foundation report search page and linked the grants to the funder's 990 report. The significance of the 990s and why we need to know about grant recipients and funders will come to bear later in this book.

What we display in our format is what a grant writer needs to know. We provide the source if they want to delve even deeper. My experience as a grant writer and our meetings with grant writers have driven our development.

For a business to be successful, it needs to solve a pain point. For grant seekers, it's the rabbit hole of the Internet, when searching for grants. Even today, with the high sophistication of the web, there are ads for supposed grants that simply take you to a page with a bunch of links to other websites. Some do not even offer a list of grants – it's the old bait and switch.

We solved that first pain point by adding new grants daily, and only displaying currently available grants with an automatic daily archive of the website and by monitoring what has changed. We review constantly, checking for updates. Because we work remotely, our hours overlap. We are always working.

Before I continue, I want to emphasize that sometimes a new feature can set you back, causing much more work for staff, for example like adding the 990s. I am grateful for the staff complaints because they made me take a step back to streamline the new process. At GrantWatch, we never sit idly by, we are always evolving to offer the best search processes and the most available information.

I have personally been involved with the development of my website, six days a week since we started 13 years ago. We have transitioned from interns to knowledgeable developers for whose loyalty, we are grateful.

My developers have always been my fingers, turning my ideas into reality. Every day we work to make the user experience better and better.

Today, we have a list of over sixty different categories, and many grants overlap categories and locations. For example: Teachers can go to the teacher category, but they can also look in the elementary school category or they can use a keyword pertaining to the subject matter. Flexibility when searching for grants works best.

My inclination is to stop and read the room to understand our subscribers' needs. With the increase of people searching for grants in 2020, we added a COVID 19 Coronavirus category. And then during the riots in Seattle and Minneapolis, we added a social justice category. A short time later the BIPOC category was also added. BIPOC stands for Black, Indigenous, People of Color. This new category provides more opportunities for the grant seeker to find funding. We also added the disaster relief category in response to the devastation of Hurricane Sandy.

Now, nonprofits have to spend a lot of time and energy to prepare a one-page synopsis of a grant application. These summaries are typically needed to be presented at a board meeting or sent through email to get people excited about joining the development team within the agency or to give their approval to apply.

Recalling my days at the DO, I knew what our synopsis of a grant, which we today call our proprietary grant detail page, needed to contain. When someone in a nonprofit or business knows of a grant they want to apply for, they must usually convince their board members to allocate funds for a grant writer. If this isn't possible, it will sometimes fall to a staff member to be reassigned for grant writing, in place of their regular responsibilities.

With GrantWatch, the employee can just download and print that synopsis of that one grant and bring it to the board meeting. The board would then review it easily and say, "Yes, this is what we want." Or "No, we're not eligible."

This is how I envisioned nonprofits and businesses using GrantWatch from the very beginning, as the first initial step towards funding. We didn't want to provide the subscriber with every single detail about each grant because we do not want to supplant the funding source's website.

We wanted to provide a one or two-page synopsis with valuable information, links to the full website, and the resources and where to find more. And if there were any addendums or something that we found that would help, we uploaded them as well.

I have always been adamant that I did not want a chop-shop of a website. We don't just cut and paste the blurb that you'll find on everybody else's website. Our staff is trained to read through the grant and pull out what is needed. Nonprofits have boards and presenting to the board shouldn't be a pain point.

Grant applications need to be reviewed for legitimacy and our grant details page for the individual grant posting needs to include the information I would, as a grant writer, want to show a client.

We went back to my original newsletter NYCGrantsWatch for reference, and we tweaked our details page a few times over the years. The pitfalls are always the possibility of information overload or what the eye wants to see first. A grant on GrantWatch is reviewed by a researcher, writer, managing editor, and proofreader, before it ever goes public.

I remember how in 2022, I was working on a new mockup of our proprietary grant detail page, adding ready facts in the left column. The thought process was to make it even easier for the grant seeker, by reorganizing our presentation.

We learn so much from our subscribers by having everyone on staff, no matter their title, engage in customer service. We found we were making everyone a bit dizzy and after months of design we revamped it again.

All our features are customer driven. I invite you to skim our top twenty features here to better understand that GrantWatch is not an island unto itself. We do not operate in a vacuum. We have evolved providing the consumer with everything they have asked for, including this book.

The 20 top current features of GrantWatch:

1. **Thousands of Currently Available Grants:** GrantWatch offers a wide range of grant opportunities with over 8,000 currently available grants and 28,000 grants in the database.

2. **Complete Grant Descriptions and Ability to Save as a PDF:** GrantWatch provides comprehensive information on grant requirements, eligibility, application process, and deadlines. Users can also save grants and their details as PDF files.

3. **Grant Eligibility with Direct Links to RFPs to Apply:** GrantWatch simplifies the grant eligibility process by highlighting key elements and providing

direct links to request for proposals (RFPs) for easy application access.

4. **Live Customer Support:** GrantWatch offers real-time customer support during business hours through phone, email, or online chat.

5. **Email Updates of the Latest Grants:** Subscribers receive weekly email updates on the latest grant opportunities, featuring the 15 most recent grants added within the last seven days in their selected location.

6. **Real-Time Personalized Grant Alerts:** Users can create personalized watchlists and receive email notifications when funders update or make changes to the grants they are interested in.

7. **Affordable Pricing Options:** GrantWatch offers affordable pricing options for both large and small nonprofits, businesses, and individuals, ensuring accessibility for everyone.

8. **Multi-User and Library Licenses:** Custom packages are available for multi-users and library licenses, allowing simultaneous access to GrantWatch for multiple users within an organization.

9. **Keep Track of Your Grant View History:** The "My Grant Views" feature keeps a record of all the grants users have viewed, including GrantWatch ID#, deadline date, and the time and date of viewing.

10. **Hide Ineligible Grants:** The "Hide Grants" feature allows users to hide irrelevant or unsuitable grants, decluttering search results and enabling focus on relevant opportunities.

11. **Personalized Grant Calendar with Submission Tracker:** The "My Grant Calendar" feature helps users plan and track upcoming grant application deadlines, improving their chances of timely submissions.

12. **Boolean Keyword Search:** GrantWatch's Boolean Keyword Search allows users to find precise grant results by using operators such as "AND," "OR," and "NOT," refining search and eliminating unwanted results.

13. **SMART Advanced Grant Search:** The SMART Advanced Search Filter enables users to search grants by recipient type, location, category interests, funding source type, and deadline date, refining their search for relevant grants.

14. **Save Your SMART Grant Search Filters:** Users can save their grant search filters to easily refer to previous search results that match their criteria, eliminating the need for repetitive searches.

15. **Foundation Search and IRS 990 Report Finder:** GrantWatch provides a Foundation Search Finder to search for foundations based on various criteria, as well as an IRS 990 Report Finder to access the financial information and activities of grant-making foundations.

16. **Grant Recipient Profiles with Reverse Search:** GrantWatch's Recipient Profiles Reverse Search helps users identify grant recipients and their funders, empowering them with valuable information for informed decisions and partnerships.

17. **Save Foundations and Recipient Search Filters:** Users can save their filters for foundation and

recipient searches, allowing them to easily revisit their search preferences.

18. **GrantNews Newsletter:** Subscribers receive a weekly newsletter featuring articles on grants, emerging trends, and recent developments in the grant world, along with grants that match their preferences.

19. **Grant Resources and Tutorial Videos:** GrantWatch provides a Grant Resources page with valuable information to assist users in their grant-seeking process, along with step-by-step tutorial videos to guide them through the platform's features.

20. **Priority Purchase of "The Queen of Grants" by Libby Hikind:** Subscribers receive an exclusive pre-order offer for Libby Hikind's book, "The Queen of Grants," providing insights and techniques for grant writing and navigating the grant-seeking process.

I am now working on reliable and responsive artificial intelligence and how it will improve the users search experience.

Just before submitting this book for publication, I took a last snippet of the website for you. 8,013 currently available grants. I invite you to go to GrantWatch.com.

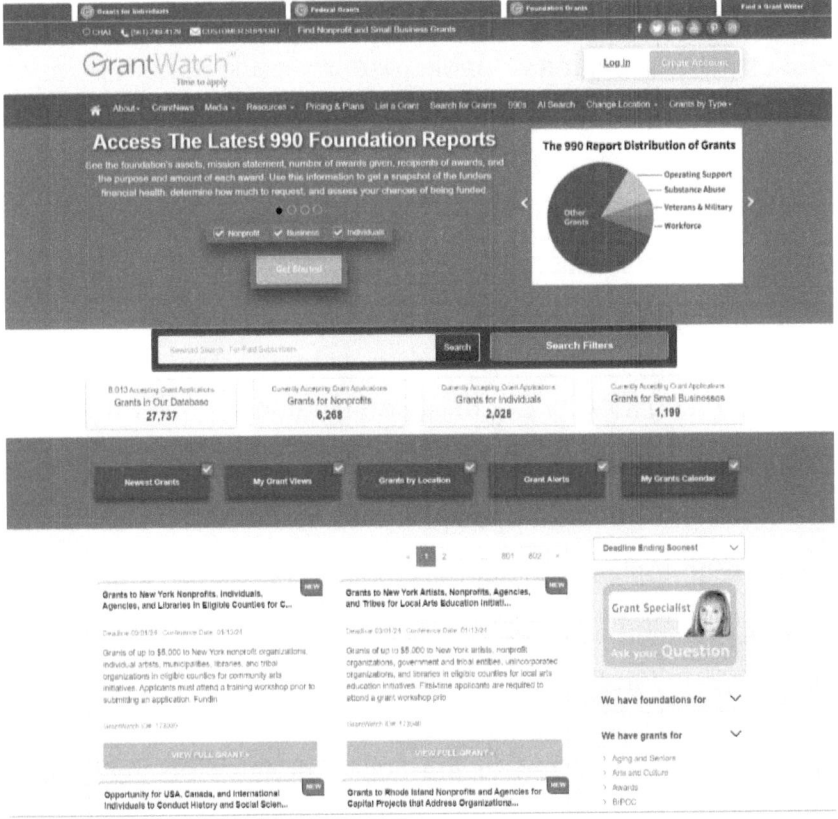

FIGURE 19: JANUARY 12TH, 2024.

A life of building blocks.

Life is a collection of building blocks, where each experience and pursuit contribute to personal growth and success. As I reflect on my previous career as a teacher of written communication skills and a grant writer, I recognize how those experiences have shaped my goals and endeavors on GrantWatch.

By leveraging my knowledge and expertise, I created a platform that provides valuable resources and opportunities to individuals and organizations seeking grants.

Just as in life, each step builds upon the previous one. By utilizing the foundation of my past experiences, I'm striving to make a positive impact within the grant-seeking community.

While running for City Council I participated in public speaking events, debates, and giving press conferences. Every endorsement I sought caused me to examine where I stood on current topics and identify solutions. Often that would involve devising a feasible budget and seeking coalitions that would join in funding support.

Now, years later, I am giving live interviews on zoom and radio. Television stations are filming me in their studio, in my house, and in my backyard. I am speaking at conferences in front of thousands of people.

Personal attention created our solid foundation.

From the very beginning, I gave every subscriber my personal attention. I wanted them to know that I empathize with their quests for funding, that I recognized their worthwhile programs, and I wanted them to succeed in finding the grant for their agencies.

I personally answered every single customer support phone call and email myself for more than two years. In the

beginning, my cell phone number was the number that was posted on the website.

My youngest daughter Lianne learned the business through osmosis. As early as her infant years, I was writing grants. When she was in her teens, GrantWatch opened.

With me answering calls day and night, at restaurants, the doctor's office, on the car speaker phone, at our dining room table, or wherever - she learned about grants and the needs of our subscribers. Lianne, now a college graduate, writes quality content articles for the website, when she is not busy writing for her many other new entrepreneurial website clients.

In our third year of operation, I finally hired someone and purchased a business phone line. Even with the new hire, I was still answering about 70% percent of the calls.

Today I am grateful to my large staff of very loyal and dedicated individuals, each with their own talents - in email marketing, content writing, social media, copy editing, customer service, grant researchers, editors, web development, and management. Together, we are a wonderfully great team.

In particular, I want to give a shout-out to the staff members that I work closely with on a daily basis: Pamela, Danika, Jon, David, Lauren, Jeff, Lianne, Christian, Alan, Nikita, Jacob, and Lori.

I want to express my gratitude to our management team, some of whom have been with the company since 2010 and others, for more than 7 years: Lani, Susan, Yaffa, Sharon, Raizel, Goldie, Pushpendra, and Shira. I am thankful for their enduring passion for the company and the work that we do, for their responsiveness to our subscribers and the quality of their work.

I still take calls occasionally, to stay in touch with the needs of subscribers. A random caller gets quite a surprise when they realize the CEO took their call. Even though I trained them, I am not as great as my staff in writing call notes and researching profiles for better assistance. My conversation always leads to business development and the big picture view of grant writing.

Challenges of a website.

One of the biggest challenges of running a website is that the internet is open 24/7. The main culture theme of my business is to provide great customer service.

To foster this theme, I believe that every staff member should respond to chats, phones, and emails as quickly as possible. We are always trying to find better ways to improve response time.

Our approach to customer service is based on the idea that we are offering a useful service at prices that are both worth the cost and affordable.

So, who is it that's calling, emailing, or chatting with us?

Executive directors of nonprofit organizations, grant writers, school principals, school district supervisors, hospital coordinators, elected officials, librarians, teachers, researchers and clergy. To me, it makes so much more sense for my educated staff to answer calls. They are the same staff who are hearing me speak, who daily, are deep in the grant world, researching and writing articles about grants. Who better to answer questions and give solid advice than the people who have become experts through years of practical experience?

Working remotely has so many challenges. Before COVID it was much easier. All calls were answered in the same office. I could always step in and help where needed. Today we are fully remote, and it has allowed committed staff members to stay on indefinitely and allowed me to hire talent from across the United States.

In the last 30 days, with all the holidays there were 230,000 unique visitors to GrantWatch. We have some subscribers that have been with us since 2010.

My aspirations for myself are to always remain personally connected to my staff and have empathy for my subscribers. And my aspirations for GrantWatch are to bring value to the nonprofit community and that every single nonprofit knows GrantWatch is available, ready, and willing to help them locate grants.

What I would tell my younger self.

In hindsight, I look back and all I got were mixed signals from professionals.

My sixth-grade career day report said I wanted to be a commercial advertising artist. My teacher loved it and felt it was the most unique report.

In college my English Composition 1.0 teacher did not like my writing and my art teacher discouraged me from a full-time art career. My parents wanted me to be a teacher or a nurse, even though I was accepted to PRATT, an art school with a portfolio submission requirement for acceptance.

I respected my parents' wishes, and I went to Brooklyn College and became a teacher with a fine arts minor. Thankfully, because I listened, I am where I am today.

I like to think that I have come full circle to commercial advertising now called marketing and have learned so much along the way.

I would have told my younger self, "Great teachers encourage and do not discourage, and if you have passion for what you are doing you will succeed!"

Today I know who I am. I am a mother, grandmother, great grandmother, wife, public speaker, retired grant writer, retired teacher and a successful CEO and entrepreneur who helps and has helped a great many people all over the world. Some call me the Queen of Grants.

I still have more ideas for expanding GrantWatch and other projects that I want to go forward with. And I may, as long as I think of my age, as only a number.

I was still writing grants.

When I created GrantWatch.com, I was still a grant writer and had many clients. I was very much in demand.

The consensus from family and friends was that I should continue to grow my grant writing business by hiring grant writers.

In 2012, five of my clients were vying for the same grant and there was more than enough funding out there for them to all be funded. They knew each other and gave consent for me to write for all five. I had won grants previously for each of these clients.

I hired five experienced grant writers, across the country, to work under my supervision. And we were not starting from scratch either. I had a lot of previously written material that could be repurposed to use inside new applications.

Unfortunately, the grant writers did not feel a deep sense of responsibility to our clientele. So, when life happened, as it always does, I was left to pick up the pieces.

One grant writer's air conditioner broke during 90-degree weather, so they could not work. Another writer's daughter experienced a medical emergency about four hundred miles away from her home. Understandably, they couldn't work either. Another had very sketchy internet in the mountains where she lived, and another's writing was simply not up to par. I ended up with one grant writer and most of the work back in my lap.

On the grant deadline date, I started receiving budgetary changes from my five clients, which then caused me to have to make changes throughout the needs statement, objectives, and activities, within each application.

Grant writers know that the budget is the foundation of any grant application. It is nearly impossible to start adding new budget items in a 100-page grant application, on the day a grant is due.

Why did I create GrantWriterTeam?

I needed to separate myself from the work of writing grants and being CEO of GrantWatch. I realized grant writers needed to be solely responsible to their clients and not to me. In my fantasy world, I imagined a do over. Amazingly enough, what I imagined became the actual blueprint for GrantWriterTeam.com.

I developed a website that allowed grant writers and grant seekers the means to cultivate productive working relationships. There was a small retainer, a set of agreed upon deliverables, timelines, and other details agreeable to both grant writer and grant seeker.

It became abundantly clear that I was onto something. The time involved in managing a grant writing business takes away time from skillful grant writing. You cannot be a grant writer and run a demanding growing grant writing business. I knew I couldn't do both well anymore, and this was the same pain point for grant writers.

My concept was to build a website that would reduce the amount of time a grant seeker spends looking for grant writing opportunities and increase their available time for writing quality grants. The new website would provide daily grant writing opportunities.

It took a year and in 2013 GrantWriterTeam was finished, and I retired from grant writing and put my full attention to running the two businesses.

Teaching Grant Writing and Public Speaking

FIGURE 21: ANNOUNCING THE FLORIDA INTERNATIONAL TRADE AND CULTURAL EXPO

I have been asked to speak at many conferences over the years from Florida to New York to Maryland and as far away as Dubai. The two most memorable were the Florida Sister Cities International Southeastern Conference in Jacksonville Florida and the Orthodox Jewish Chamber of Commerce in Manhattan.

In September 2017, I was asked by Duvi Honig, Founder and CEO of the OJC, Orthodox Jewish Chamber of Commerce to be a panelist for the Empowering Women in the Workforce session at the NY Hilton.

FIGURE 22: ANNOUNCING THE WOMEN IN THE WORKFORCE CONFERENCE OF THE ORTHODOX JEWISH CHAMBER OF COMMERCE.

I presented together with Rachel Van Tosh the Deputy Commissioner of NYC Department of Small Business and

Services, and Rebecca Harary, an entrepreneur and founder of Propel Network for women entering the workforce.

The OJC's mission, to unite the world through commerce was palpable in the diverse audience. Rachel, Rebecca and I presented and fielded lightning-fast questions about workforce initiatives, opportunities for women, small business grants, and the state of the economy

Donna Scantlebury contacted me. Donna is the Florida State Representative for Sister Cities International, and she asked if I would teach, together with Karol Mason, the CEO of A Word to the Wise, a Grant Writing Economic Empowerment Workshop. I was totally on board.

We structured the workshop into two parts. Grant writing training and a grant writing competition.

Ten annual subscriptions to GrantWatch would be the awards. Each of the ten cities whose proposals showed thought and promise would receive an annual subscription to GrantWatch. In the second session, each Sister City would submit their brief proposal form in writing and pitch their innovative program. The other Sister Cities and myself and Karol asked questions, based on the first session and to clarify and critique their program. It was a productive brainstorming session, hearing about the needs and goals of cities from all over the world.

FIGURE 23: ANNOUNCING THE SISTERCITIES INTERNATIONAL CONFERENCE

FIGURE 24: KAROL MASON, CEO A WORD TO THE WISE; LIBBY HIKIND, FOUNDER & CEO OF GRANTWATCH; DONNA SCANTLEBURY, SISTER CITIES INTERNATIONAL FLORIDA STATE REPRESENTATIVE; AND BRENDA FRINKS, PRESIDENT OF JACKSONVILLE SISTER CITIES ASSOCIATION, INC.

While conferences temporarily distract projects that I am working on, a conference where I have a public speaking engagement energizes me and ignites an additional level of passion. The pre-announcement instills a sense of pride among my staff. And the connection with individuals who need GrantWatch services during these events reinforces the significance of our work. I return with renewed enthusiasm and congratulations for my staff.

There are future Sister Cities conferences on the horizon that I look forward to speaking at.

The start and sale of YouHelp.com

YouHelp had multiple domain names before we settled upon youhelp.com. I developed and redeveloped the website so many times. By December 2022, it was a crowdfunding website for verified nonprofits, with an IRS final letter of determination, clearly stating that they were a nonprofit 501(c)3.

YouHelp's first name was GrantsWE.fund, which no one could understand on the phone, GrantsWe.com, which was still confusing, Uhelp.com which we had to explain was spelled like U-Haul and finally I found YouHelp.com. After many months, I tracked down the owners and bought the domain.

With the many transformations of YouHelp.com, I consistently felt I was failing when all I'd ever done, my whole life, was try my hardest to succeed. Crowdfunding was not my area of expertise.

My family and friends were ever so tired of hearing me say next month, next month it would be better. If I could just solve this or that, I know it will be a success. This had been going on since 2016 and I would not let it go. I kept putting in hours and effort. I believed in my heart of hearts I could make it work through perseverance and hard work.

Six years later, YouHelp had yet to support itself or become profitable, but it helped so many people. Every time I set a date to close it, the website would get a new promising campaign and then it would fizzle out. I did not have the heart to close it. I started to look for a buyer. The few people I approached said the website had little value. I finally sold it for peanuts in December 2022 and I got out of the crowdfunding industry.

Work-life balance

In August 2022, I was packing for a long drive to Tampa, a four-hour ride to be interviewed live, on Bloom TV on WTTA Great 38 - Tampa. This was the first time I would go in-person to a television station. After all, I'd spent the last three years of COVID doing numerous TV interviews on Zoom or with the TV News filming in my office or backyard.

My PR company, Hey Sandy! PR & Communications told me that TV stations were moving away from Zoom interviews, and I was requested to be at their studio.

To prepare, I needed a capable staff member to compile the list of the available grants in Tampa and surrounding areas. It was a long ride, and I wanted to click back and forth on my cell phone and review for the interview. I always try to anticipate the questions and store data in my brain so I can feel prepared.

I received this message back from a staff member who was managing the project: "I have someone else working on the spreadsheet now in order to make the changes. Today is my 42nd wedding anniversary so I am meeting my husband for our day out together. I will be offline with travel and lunch for the next 5 hours. You should be able to see the changes on the sheet. I will check before I go, and I'll go online when I get home and check again. I will touch base with you later."

This response was perfectly reasonable. But I was stressed and channeling my inner Miranda Priestly from The *Devil Wears Prada*. I was ready to bark, but I didn't!

My reaction was atypical because I felt envy. Forty-two years is a milestone, but I was more envious that the staff member had work-life balance.

I wrote back, "Wishing you much happiness and Mazal (good luck) and Kol Hakavod (honor) to you, that you have work life balance. I have yet to achieve that in my life."

And her response? "Thanks so much, not always easy but always a priority."

My advice to entrepreneurs.

And so that is my **first** piece of advice to other entrepreneurs. It is not easy to achieve a work-life balance. However, never give up trying to achieve it, and don't sacrifice one part of your life for the other. No one loves a martyr, and therefore you will never be happy.

Try to make it work and let your family know how you are trying. Make all the plans you need with colleagues and clients at work but keep your home life separate. Take time for family, friends, and most importantly, yourself.

My **second** piece of advice is your career should always be about doing what you know. Build on your existing knowledge base, feel passionate about what you are doing, and you will continue to learn and grow.

The one website that never became a success under my tutelage was YouHelp.com. That is because in theory and practice YouHelp works, but I personally do not enjoy asking people to donate to a cause and I do not have experience fundraising for nonprofits. I am a teacher and a grant writer. I am a tither and a giver. Having needed help from others many years ago, I work extremely hard to never be in that position again.

My two runs for elected office had me on the phone asking for campaign contributions for half of every day, and it was the absolute worst part of the campaign. When I had to raise money, not as a candidate, but for something in the community, I ended up donating the amount myself, even when it was a difficult amount to afford.

I sold YouHelp.com to an entrepreneur with crowdfunding experience, for a pittance and included a lot of domains in the sale. It was the end of our fiscal year, and I was not going to pay the corporation fee and other renewals into 2023. The contract process took forever, and the move to another server was painfully tedious. I had hoped that with his experience he would work on the website, and I would have another legacy. However, a substantial amount of time has passed and as of today, the website still exists on the web, pretty much as we left it. Campaigns are still there, but when sold we disconnected all existing campaigns from our payment processors. This wasn't the legacy I had expected when I made the sale.

My **third** piece of advice is about borrowing money. This advice is for the reader, my children, and my grandchildren.

I built GrantWatch without borrowing money. I used some of the funds as they came in from grant writing and I worked slowly and deliberately and returned money back into the business. Until my daughter and I could operate and draw some revenue for a salary, we worked without it. Initially, we did everything ourselves without hiring.

I would not advise anybody to borrow a lot of money to go into business. That is how businesses fail. Don't borrow money. You have an idea? Start small.

For example, if you want to be a grant writer, you do not need the most up-to-date computer. You need writing skills and a computer with a strong internet connection, Word, Excel, PowerPoint, and a thumb drive to back up your work and research. That's it!

Many great businesses started in a garage. Anybody who is serious will clear out their garage or basement or work from their bedroom because they have passion. I have worked and written in all those spaces.

Those are the businesses that succeed.

I never needed a magnificent workspace or a lot of gadgets on my desk. The clutter would totally distract me. I do not let the minutia stand in my way. I look at the big picture of what I want to accomplish and by when.

That's how I work and lead. I also have the ability to adapt and I'm able to use this talent proactively.

Just today, I spilled a full 12-ounce cup of coffee on my relatively new Surface laptop while editing this book. The computer is now toast! I am now writing and working and running my company on a smaller, older laptop, without even taking the time to order the replacement. I set my sights on a deadline, and inch by inch, I am going to make it.

I tell you this because this is how you succeed!

If you must always have the latest newest gadget, then you're not going anywhere. You're just getting caught up in small things and you are not seeing the forest from the trees.

My **fourth** piece of advice is to start small, have your idea, and always have an eye on the big picture. There is one thing I didn't realize; I did not conceive of how great GrantWatch was really going to be. I never thought that GrantWatch was going to become a national and international phenomenon. I didn't see that.

When I started building, I also didn't know that much about coding, even though I did learn a little bit by studying and teaching my class. We had the concept and lots of spaghetti code and had to redo as we grew.

My **fifth** piece of advice is to make all changes in small increments. GrantWatch.com is much more beautiful and functional today than when we first started. But it worked then, and people found grants. Today, whenever someone new comes on board, they have these lofty ideas of how to make it better. While change is always good, small steps are best.

How do you feel when your bank updates their website, or your grocery store reorganizes their shelves? It's frustrating. When you are used to something existing one way and suddenly somebody changes your tools, it challenges your sense of control.

I never want our subscribers to feel confused and upset after using our services. I always ask my people to make small, high value, positive changes to the front end. And, of course, by front end, I mean there are two kinds of development, front and back. The backend is what the developer sees; the front is for users. So, changes made for subscribers need to be exceedingly small, so it doesn't interrupt the flow of research.

It is all about being resourceful and not about the lack of resources. Using what is available to make something great.

I believe that many of us could achieve so much more if we focused on what we know, where our passions lie, and built upon that a little bit at a time, to move forward.

The last straw for GrantWriterTeam

Why did I want to close a profitable business? Our accountant tells me no one ever does that! Every day, there seemed to be a new obstacle course concerning contracted work between grant writers and grant seekers, new problems to solve, and issues to resolve. But really, it just wasn't making me happy anymore.

When we built GrantWriterTeam it was to have a small retainer and a set of deliverables, paid to the grant writer through our portal, when work was completed. People did not follow the rules and would sometimes request payment for work not yet completed or a client who didn't want to be bothered would pay off-site of the website in one lump sum. Subsequently, it would come back to haunt everyone.

My staff has been through a lot of horror stories trying to manage both sides of the grant writing experience, including grant writers taking large retainers and then becoming uncommunicative, or grant seekers who do not pay after work is completed.

I remember one year when a grant writer took on so much work that she broke down, and we had to track down family members to refund her clients.

Another time, we had a grant writer who did not complete his work. We called his references and finally found him and arranged for several refunds.

One morning, my day started with an argument between a client who wanted a refund and the grant writer who owns a successful grant writing company. The grant writer offered a pretty large partial refund, to make him happy. The client refused. The client then went on to malign everyone on social media. When I looked the client up in our system, I found copies of additional abusive emails that he had sent to the grant writer.

I speak across the country about the importance of following directions and meeting eligibility criteria. When there is a disconnect between grant writers and clients, it usually ends with my customer service staff getting bogged down with refunds and angry clients.

In early April 2023, after running GrantWriterTeam for about 10 years, the last straw came for us all when a grant seeker claimed to be a nonprofit and had their grant writer develop a program. However, when it was time to submit the documents, it turned out this individual was not actually a nonprofit and was instead part of an umbrella organization.

Despite this, they insisted that the grant be submitted as though they were the 501(c)3 and if they win the grant, for the check to be written directly to them.

How did the grant writer miss not getting the IRS Letter of Determination, early on? She had asked multiple times. And why did the client believe that the grant writer would submit the application on their behalf?

I have always instructed grant writers to not submit on behalf of the client. If the submission is too complicated for the client to submit, then only submit, using the client's company email address.

The grant writer called me in a panic, saying that the client wanted her to submit false information, which she refused to do. He paid for the work but continued to insist. I'm proud to say, she stood firm and refused to break the law.

I guided the grant writer through her frustration with her difficult client. Of course, my response was to tell her not to submit the grant on behalf of the client. Instead, she should provide him with the grant application narrative and budget that he paid for, and to explain in writing, why he was unlikely to get funded if he pretended to be a nonprofit when he was not. I also strongly suggested to her to inform her client in writing that he should have the fiscal sponsor be the applicant and prepare an (MOU) memorandum of understanding with the umbrella organization regarding their administrative costs.

I started noticing that the more popular GrantWriterTeam became, the more customer service calls pertaining to GrantWriterTeam were jamming us up and bringing down company morale. No one likes to live through the break-up of two parties.

We had no control over the grant writer's work or the grant seeker's satisfaction. Add to that, we were dealing with the payments that went through our portal, and the chargebacks were affecting our accounts.

While I appreciated that the majority of our grant writers had won many grants and helped countless organizations secure funding, I needed to protect my staff. They were tied up with minutiae. They were dealing with arguments between contracted grant writers and clients, and the liability to our main website was just too great for something that I had no control over.

Unfortunately, when a client doesn't win a grant, the first place they point the finger at is the grant writer. It's only natural to let your disappointment find a target.

We advise all our subscribers that winning a grant is never guaranteed. Even with the most well-crafted grant there is still an element of chance. I also always advise grant writers to keep a record of all their communications with the client. This protects them as well as their client.

Even though there are countless factors that come into play when a grant is awarded or rejected, the GrantWriterTeam client would sometimes decide that they want a refund. Regardless of how many times we would explain that grants are not guaranteed, and that all questions must be fully answered, some clients simply cannot accept it.

We developed a new business model for GrantWriterTeam.

We temporarily closed GrantWriterTeam in April 2023 and re-opened it in July 2023 with a new business model.

When we closed we allowed grant writers and grant seekers to work together off our website and told them we held no responsibility if they had issues.

I was fully ready to close GrantWriterTeam, but the outcry was too loud. Good grant writers needed work. Some had been with us since 2013 and the GrantWatch subscribers wanted to know where to find a grant writer.

What we did was change the business model where GrantWriterTeam would only be a listing or advertising website. We require certain information from the grant writer and grant seeker to be public and we only collect payment for the advertising use of our platform.

Many disclaimers later, we let everyone know buyer beware and we are totally hands off and out of the "dating service" between grant seeker and grant writer.

GrantWriterTeam is not a money-making website. It is a service to the grant industry. We are no longer in a situation where we receive chargebacks and daily complaints.

When we receive a complaint, we question both sides and as per our terms and conditions, we remove either the grant writer or grant seeker from the website. It is not always as easy as it sounds when there is a complaint, but it is 100% better than before.

GrantWriterTeam has new classified ads advertising grant writer jobs daily and new grant seekers are continuously joining or leaving the listing, depending on their workload. The jobs are posted from one to four weeks, so the grant writer is not chasing rainbows.

We took ourselves out of the equation in the new business model. We have more time for our GrantWatch subscribers, and my staff is a much happier team!

II: Your Questions Answered

I have prepared this section in anticipation of all your questions. The questions I chose to include are the most common questions from thirteen years of customer service phone calls, interviews, and conferences, where I have served as a facilitator or guest speaker.

What is a grant?

A grant is a gift, an award of money, or in-kind goods or services support. It does not need to be paid back to the funding source. A grant is given when your application scores high enough to be funded, according to how much money is available and how many grants the organization plans to award.

Grants can be a great funding source to implement services within the community. New grants are published every day. Grants are gifts. They're not loans and they can originate from both the public sector and private sources.

Grants can help you, your family, your school, your nonprofit, your business, your community, and the world.

How do I receive a grant?

You receive a grant by writing a proposal. The proposal may be as short as a one-page online questionnaire to well over 100 pages, plus attachments.

The length and questions of an application are decided by the funding source and often relate to the scale of funding they are willing to award. It is common practice to say, "I am writing a grant," or "I am writing a grant proposal," or "I am completing a grant application."

Grant writing is the mother of invention. Only when you or your organization really needs a grant will you perfect, and perfect it, until you feel it is complete!

When a funding source (a grant making agency) officially announces that grant funds are available for a project, they release one of these: an RFP request for proposals, an RFA request for applications, RFI request for information, or RFQ request for qualifications. While government agencies tend to categorize, a foundation may simply call it a grant application.

Most often the format for submitting a grant application will include the needs statement, organizational history, mission/vision, goals, objectives, activities, timeline, key staff, evaluation and a budget and a budget narrative. Each one of these will be explained in greater detail in the third section of this book.

Where do grants come from?

Sometimes the funding source is the federal, state, city, or local government. Other times, it's a family trust, a philanthropist, or the foundation of a corporation, or the corporation themselves that is giving the grant.

With the on-set of COVID and now with inflation, we find new funding sources participating in grant giving from industry specific organizations or companies that produce products, wanting to provide for the people that use their products. I remember during COVID we came across a grant for hair salons that was coming from the shampoo maker Pantene. Grants come from a variety of sources. New grants are offered and posted daily on GrantWatch.

Do I have to pay back a grant?

Grants are a gift. They do not have to be paid back when you have documented that you completed everything that you proposed you would do, used the funds appropriately according to the budget and proposal narrative; and you have met all of the expectations and requirements of the funding source.

When you write a grant proposal, you are saying, this is exactly how you are going to spend the money, if awarded. The funder may require things like midpoint and endpoint reports or summative and formative evaluations. If so, these must all be submitted on time.

The funding source may also schedule a visit to view your program in action and make recommendations for improvements and/or request a report. Any proposed budgetary changes must also be submitted for approval.

I want to preface this next part with something: I am not providing nor am I qualified to give any accounting or financial advice. Your nonprofit must have a CPA familiar with nonprofit laws and regulations on your staff or contracted with. What I'm giving you here is my sound advice from lessons I've learned and obstacles I've overcome throughout the years.

While a grant is a gift, the grant recipient must include the amount of the grant and information on the nonprofit's IRS 990 form. A nonprofit's 990s are public on the IRS website. Additionally, the funder may also publicize grants they have given, as it is good PR for them.

There are very stiff penalties when an organization does not file their 990 forms in a timely fashion. A nonprofit can even lose their tax-exempt status. If your nonprofit status is revoked, that too will become public knowledge and you will be less likely to receive future grant funding.

One thing I feel is of utmost importance when you are awarded a grant is that you open a separate checking account under the name of the grant recipient: the organization, business, or individual. This account should only be used for approved expenditures related to the grant-funded program..

Keep all the receipts and show that you've spent every single penny according to the approved budget. You never want to have to return a grant or be prosecuted or go to jail for mishandling funds.

Forgivable loans are loans that may turn into a grant. With COVID there came this new funding type. These loans were given out to anyone who was eligible and completed their application correctly. Providing that the businesses followed the requirements, the loan would become forgivable. The most well-known of these was the PPP Paycheck Protection Program.

My accountant completed the paperwork for two of our companies/websites and we received the funds. I returned the funds on the day the money arrived in our accounts.

There was so much uncertainty and anxiety at that time. Would it really be forgivable and if not, did I want my business to take on debt in a time of economic stress?

People were in a crisis financially with all the shuttering of businesses and large numbers of deaths were being reported daily.

We had published 1,000 new COVID grant opportunities and saw the money run out almost as quickly as we posted. I felt the money should go to people who needed it more. We lost friends, as well.

In hindsight, it was probably a mistake to return the money. The PPP was designed to be a direct incentive for small businesses to keep the workers on payroll. If you did that, and you filed the papers accordingly, it was to be forgiven, which means you don't have to pay it back.

With a forgivable loan that you apply for and accept, you are saying that you're going to spend the money in the manner that is required by the funding agency, and if you meet all the requirements, that loan will turn into a grant.

The forgivable loans information for the PPP was initially very confusing and with an increase in people coming to our website, I felt it was wrong to accept the money.

My banker told me that at that time, with all the uncertainty, other companies also immediately returned the funds. Good to know, I was not alone in my actions.

Loans do have to be paid back. When you get a loan, you are borrowing money at a rate of interest for a specific number of payments over a period of a specific number of years. Some loans can be paid back early without a penalty and others may have one. Read the fine print. And always try not to borrow money!

Can I include a grant writer's salary in the budget?

When you write a grant, you create a proposed budget. And in that budget, you must map out how every single dollar will be allocated in accordance with the requirements of the funding source. The funding source usually indicates what it will and will not pay for.

I do not remember seeing a grant where the funding source allows paying a grant writer (except in the rare case of capacity building).

If the nonprofit has a general support budget, or they raised additional funds through donations, they can pay the grant writer from those funds with board approval.

Grant writers know that there are many reasons why a client is not funded and working on consignment or spec is an unbelievably bad business practice. It is also looked at as possibly illegal and at a minimum, unethical.

About 30 years ago, I was approached by a curriculum group to write a grant that was due in 4 days. They were going to write me into the budget for professional development to train teachers in their curriculum.

If they got the grant, I would have a great second job. There is an expression, "If it sounds too good to be true, it probably is."

The caveat was that they did not have any funds to compensate me to write the grant. It was a sure thing because it was exactly what they do, and I was young and thought, what do I have to lose?

I lost a lot of sleep. I was teaching and worked each night all the way through to the morning.

Of course, they did not get the grant, because they were missing required paperwork, and could not get it signed in time, but they did get my grant. How so? Because now they had a professionally written application that they could use repeatedly, tweak the parts to be applicable to the next application and I GOT NOTHING! Never heard from them again.

When a company is grateful and wants to show appreciation with a bonus, after they have paid your fee and not from the grant funds, that's fine. A bonus should never be given in advance as that will look like money for influence peddling.

Do not put yourself in a position where you are paid solely on commission. First, it doesn't make sense because the scoring of a grant is subjective and based upon many factors besides excellent writing. The eligibility criteria and applicant's history are what is put under the microscope. If they don't match the funder's intent for the programs to be funded, no amount of clever phrasing will win that grant.

And secondly, you never want to be in a position where you are trying to contact every connection you know to push your grant. Working on commission makes you want to ensure that your client wins the grant and incentivizes you to lobby on their behalf. Leave that to the client and let your work stand on its merits.

While I am not an attorney, here are my thoughts. This is not legal advice, and you should consult a nonprofit attorney.

I don't believe it is unethical or illegal to give a salaried W-2 employee a bonus from funds not related to the grant. That is, if this is the usual practice for your staff to get merit bonuses and the employee is fully compensated for their work through their regular salary.

The employee should have no prior connection to the funding source. This minimizes the possibility of influence peddling to get the bonus. You need to be careful not to incentivize staff to lobby to receive a bonus.

Is it difficult to apply for grants?

It depends on which grant you're applying for. A grant could be small, it could be one page online with just a few brief questions. Or it could be 100 pages, it really depends on the funding source, and who they're funding and what they're planning to fund. The smaller the grant, the less difficult it will be. That's usually a rule of thumb.

How to avoid grant scams?

Remember that you need to apply for a grant. Nobody will ever just give you a grant; no one will call you up and say, "Hey, you just won a grant!"

This is not how it works. You need to apply for a grant and complete everything as the funding source requested. There'll be a period while the decision is being made, and you'll get an award letter in the mail. There will be a phone number for the foundation or government agency that you can verify. You will be in contact with people who can be verified.

Do not speak to someone calling you from a call center that tells you that you won a grant and to send them money for the taxes before receiving the grant through a cash app, gift card, Green Dot, Western Union, or any other form of payment. These are scams and the money you send them will never be seen again. What's worse? The information they mine from you during this scam may also be sold or kept for future use. What's even worse? There is virtually no way to track the culprits.

When you receive an email, hover your mouse over the email address to see the real email address it is coming from. Companies funding grants use their business name dot com or dot org, not a Gmail or AOL account.

Again, "If it sounds too good to be true, it is!"

On the bottom of GrantWatch we have a disclaimer:

GrantWatch is a secure search and listing directory of currently available grants, accepting grant applications.

We only charge a small subscription fee to use our service. GrantWatch does not give grants, rather, we grant access to grants that clients may then apply for.

Never pay an imposter who asks you to purchase a gift card, or pre-pay money for a guaranteed grant, or to give money-back for a grant, or to send a check.

What are the 990s?

GrantWatch has now included a button on the grant detail page, the feature of "View 990 Report."

Form 990 is an IRS filing required by foundations issuing grants. It contains valuable information for grant writers and is publicly accessible. The 990 provides contact details such as address, phone number, and website of the foundation. Additionally, it reveals the foundation's tax form submission calendar, allowing estimation of when the latest 990 will be available.

The 990 report also discloses the fair market value of the foundation's assets and their distribution. This information is crucial for understanding the foundation's minimum award requirement, as the IRS mandates a 5% distribution of the average market value of investments and assets. Failure to meet this requirement results in the payment of an excise tax.

Furthermore, the 990 lists the foundation's board members along with their contact information. Grant writers can leverage platforms like LinkedIn to connect with them. Notably, board members may receive compensation in the form of a stipend or an allocation of grant funds. This arrangement gives them the authority to make unrestricted grants to charities they strongly support, rather than receiving a cash stipend for their board service.

There are three types of 990 forms, and certain types provide specific information about grants. These forms can identify the total amount of grants awarded by the foundation, the recipients of those grants, as well as the specific grant awards and their purposes. This information is invaluable for grant writers seeking to understand the foundation's grant-making history, priorities, and focus areas. By analyzing this data, grant writers can tailor their proposals to align with the foundation's interests and increase their chances of securing funding.

What 990 information is helpful?

While the 990s may be difficult to read, GrantWatch has zeroed in on what a grant writer needs to know about an organization. All the information provided helps the organization determine if a nonprofit should apply for a grant from this organization based on their funding history and their amount of assets, purposes for which they have funded, and the dollar value of grants given.

The Overview page for a foundation on GrantWatch gives you the legal name for the organization, its mission statement (as provided to the IRS), legal address phone number, and the organization's URL.

Additionally, it will provide you with the codes that categorize the organizations: NTEE Code, Tax Code, EIN, Subsection code, Asset Code, Affiliation Code and Deductibility Code.

All the codes are defined on the IRS website.

https://www.irs.gov/pub/irs-tege/p4838.pdf

Most importantly on the Overview page are two bar graphs illustrating the past years – as far back as 2015 through 2023 -- the dollar value of the grants they provided to others (outgoing – awarded to others), and the dollar value of grants that the foundation has received (incoming – awards received).

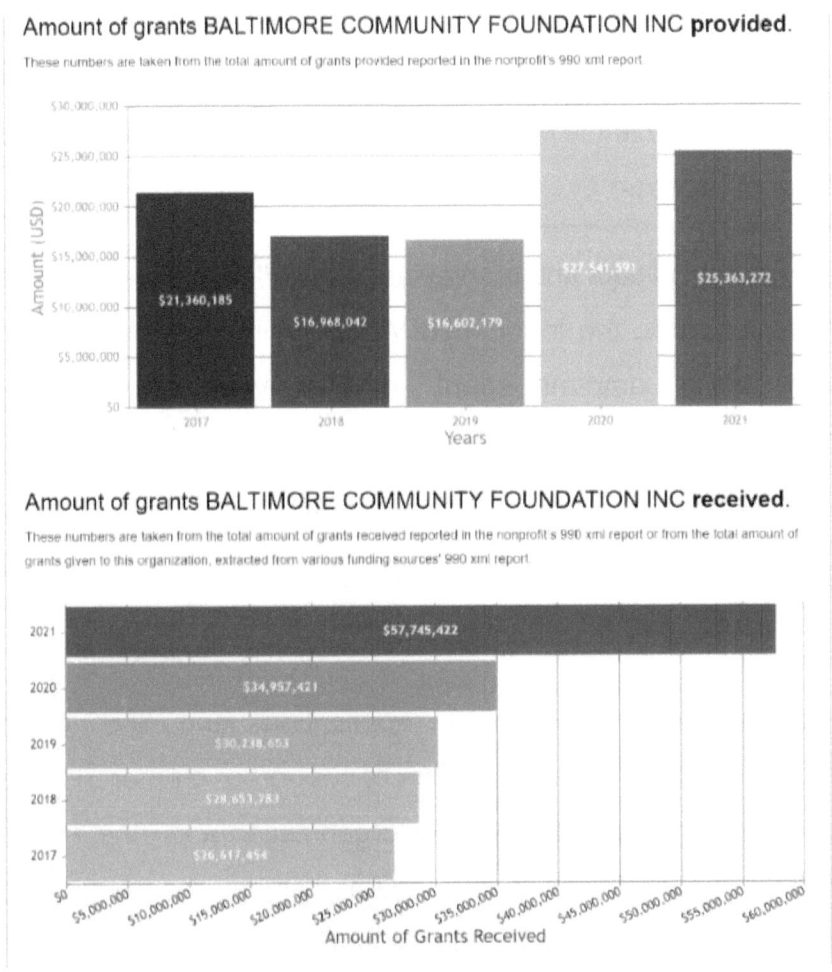

FIGURE 25: FROM IRS 990 REPORTS.

The information on GrantWatch is extracted from the nonprofit's 990 xml report and provided to subscribers, in an easy-to-understand pictorial format.

Each year shown on the Overview page has a corresponding individual annual page that contains a partial listing of grants awarded: the name of the organization that they awarded, the address, the purpose of the award, and the amount of the grant award given. In the grants received section we list the funder who gave the grant, their location, the purpose, and the amount received by the organization.

We list key officers and employees, their titles and weekly time commitment to the foundation. Additionally, you will see the total dollar amount spent in that year on salaries, compensation, and benefits.

How long does it take to write a grant?

The length of time to write a grant is dependent upon the questions within the application and the grant requirements. If you need letters of support or memorandums of understanding between your organization and others, that can jam up your time. If you need any signatures from board members or government officials that too will hold you up.

Research into best practices, meetings with organizational staff, and budgetary numbers, etc., are all time consuming and interrupts the writing flow. The longer the amount of lead time before the deadline, the better your application will be.

However, if a grant is right for your organization, then put in those late nights and get it done, if possible. Do not miss an opportunity.

How much does it cost to hire a grant writer?

The cost of hiring a grant writer depends on the scope and complexity of the grant application.

I like to use the analogy of calling a painter on the phone and asking him how much he will charge to paint your living quarters. He will then ask you a few questions about the size of your home, the square footage of the property, are there pictures or furniture to move? Do you want to paint a studio above a garage? Or a 12-room mansion?

No one can answer the question of the cost of hiring a grant writer, because there are no standard costs. Grant writing is not a standardized industry.

What you should develop with a grant writer is a contract with a small retainer and a set of deliverables and deadlines. Be truly clear as to what you want them to accomplish in each deliverable and you can pay for each when the work is done.

Without knowing what specific grant application you're looking at, and the specific requirements of the submission, no one should be able to respond to this question.

The full grant detail page on GrantWatch is available beyond the paywall and helps grant seekers determine whether they can handle the application on their own or if they need assistance from a grant writer.

On GrantWatch, the basic Member gets you on our email list and you can view a very brief promo of each grant.

The MemberPlus subscribers have access to the entire GrantWatch website with all the grant details and search capabilities, including detailed eligibility criteria, and the link to the application on the grant funders website.

You'll get a feeling as to whether the application is something that qualifies as, "I can apply for that on my own." or "This is way above my background and expertise. I need to hire a grant writer."

The length and complexity of grant applications can vary significantly. Some applications may be as simple as a one-page online form with checkboxes, while others may require filling in paragraphs or even have specific word counts for each section. The difficulty sometimes is in conveying all the necessary information within the given constraints.

The federal government provides a suggested number of hours for completing their applications, giving applicants an idea of the time commitment needed.

Ultimately, the cost of hiring a grant writer depends on the specific funder's requirements and the expertise and time needed to complete it effectively.

When hiring a grant writer, don't be shy. Ask for one page writing samples from each grant that piques your interest. Ask for and check their references. Find out how the grant writer's background matches with the subject of your grant application.

Grant writers who advertise on GrantWriterTeam are asked to provide writing samples and references and they have the ability to make it public, when asked for you to review. They do this to establish trust and showcase their talents.

We do not vet the grant writers. We leave that to the grant seekers to check references and writing samples. It's been my experience in the past that you should be wary of anyone who cannot provide you with samples of their work and references.

One thing I always tell grant seekers is to write your first grant by yourself. I advise grant seekers to start by writing a smaller grant application. Don't write a tremendous one, you'll get frustrated, you'll never submit it. Select a small grant application and write it yourself.

You'll be gathering up all that information that you need. And you will get a sense of what's needed to write a grant even if you don't succeed. And not every grant application gets funded.

When I went to Washington, D.C., to read grants for the federal government, they were giving out 40 grants and had received about 1,000 submissions.

I would say a great majority of grants received scores in the 90s. But only the top 40 got funded. So, don't feel bad if you don't win, not every application can get funded. Your second grant will be so much better and easier to write because you'll have all those documents ready at your fingertips.

Every grant proposal a grant seeker submits serves as their foundation for future applications. My advice? You should always ask for and obtain the reviewer's notes. They will provide a basis for improvement and streamlining the preparation of your next application.

Should I hire a grant writer?

Writing your first grant yourself allows you to gather all the necessary information, which takes time and preparation. Just like painting a house, you need to invest effort into preparing the walls and windows to ensure a smooth finish. Similarly, preparing the documents and writing the grant proposal can be time-consuming but greatly worth the effort. It is an opportunity to gather all the required information in one place.

I have two recommendations. One, don't sweat it. You will do your best and learn a great deal along the way. Two – no matter what grant you apply for, try to make it a small one. Get your feet wet. The grant is going to get you to gather all your documentation inside your grant ready folder.

Keep in mind, sometimes it takes longer to prepare all the documents than to write your proposal.

And if you're successful, go on, and write your next grant. I was successful. I became a grant writer. Nobody knows what their hidden talents are. Somebody that sells cars is successful because they sell with words. A grant writer is selling what the organization wants to do, with words.

If you are not successful, then hire a grant writer. Most of the time, people are thrilled with their grant writers, and they continue to go on and on and build the organization together.

Can you apply for grants while your IRS tax-exempt status is pending?

Most funding sources require a final letter of determination from the IRS, which is proof of your organization's nonprofit status. This means that you won't be able to apply while your tax-exempt status is pending unless you team up with another nonprofit, as your fiscal sponsor or as the lead organization in a consortium application.

The IRS says that you should expect to hear from them within 180 days after submitting your Form 1023 application. However, this often takes much longer, with some organizations reporting up to a year of waiting.

If you do not have 501(c)3 nonprofit status here is the current URL to apply:

https://www.irs.gov/charities-non-profits/charitable-organizations

Are there grants for small businesses?

There are grants for small businesses. It's a common misconception that the only way to win a grant is if you have a 501(c)(3) nonprofit status.

There are less grants for small businesses. However, since COVID, we've seen an increase in small business and individual grants. With COVID we saw a lot come through the SBA, the EIDL, the Economic Injury Disaster Loans - Small Business Administration, the PPP, the Payroll Protection Program, the shuttered venue grants for movie theaters, restaurants, the entertainment industry and now the ERC tax credit. State and local government agencies are supporting small businesses with grants as well. I think there will be more and more grants available for individuals and small businesses from local government agencies as well as from the federal government.

The first thing when it comes to business, is don't look at a grant as something that will save you. If you adopt the attitude that there will be a large influx of cash to your business, it may lead to overspending or fiscal mismanagement. Do not recklessly spend money because you apply for a grant. To stay in business, you really must manage your business well, and that includes the purse strings.

Years ago, I had a staff member I really liked, and I was in awe of her creativity. I felt at the time that she could help me grow the company to the next level. My staff was working out of a three-room space adapted with folding tables, chairs and lots of computer equipment and phones.

This staff member was approached through LinkedIn by another company. She told me of their equity offer and their beautiful multi-floor space with the latest video game box, ping pong tables, swings, pool tables, and how they wanted their staff to relax and be creative.

I offered her a raise to stay, but I wasn't able to compete with their indoor playground and the equity in the business they were promising.

Furthermore, I told her that with me she would always have a job. With them, not so sure. The way they were spending money made me tell her, "A percentage of zero is still zero."

I gave her my opinion, "GrantWatch will be around because we are fiscally responsible. We do not operate on debt. We do not over-extend and when we spend money, we are careful to spend within the limits of our revenue."

They were out of business in less than 6 months, and she was out of a job and had no equity. We had already hired her replacement.

Waiting to win a grant can have much the same effect. When you receive a letter about a grant that you applied for and won, DO NOT start spending money. Wait for the funds, stick to a budget. A grant for a small business is the cream of the crop, the cherry on the top of the work that is your ice cream sundae. It is going to help your business retrofit or expand or do something of value. If you run your business to the ground, spending and spending, no grant will save you.

Should we become a charity?

It really depends on what your goals are. If you want to make money and you are entrepreneurial, a nonprofit is not who you want to be.

If you want to accept donations and serve the community for the greater good, then apply for your 501(c)3 nonprofit status and become a public charity.

There are many other 501(c) statuses you can explore with your attorney and CPA. Most grants are available to 501(c)3 nonprofit organizations, however other statuses have been eligible and have received grants.

501(c)(1): Corporations Organized Under Act of Congress

501(c)(3): Charitable, Religious or Educational Organizations

501(c)(4): Community Social Welfare Organizations

501(c)(5), 501(c)(16): Labor, Agricultural and Horticultural Organizations and Cooperative Organizations to Finance Crop Organizations

501(c)(6): Business Leagues

501(c)(7), 501(c)(8), 501(c)(10): Lodges, Fraternities, Societies and Recreation Clubs

501(c)(9): Voluntary Employees' Beneficiary Associations

501(c)(11): Teachers' Retirement Fund Associations

501(c)(12), 501(c)(15), 501(c)(26), 501(c)(29): Insurance and Services at Cost

501(c)(13): Cemetery Companies

501(c)(14): State-Chartered Credit Unions and Other Mutual Financial Organizations

501(c)(17), 501(c)(18), 501(c)(22): Pensions and Unemployment Trusts

501(c)(19), 501(c)(23): Veterans Organizations Before and After 1880

501(c)(21): Black Lung Benefit Trusts

501(c)(27): State-Sponsored Workers' Compensation Organizations

501(c)(28): National Railroad Retirement Investment Fund

501(d): Religious and Apostolic Associations

501(e): Cooperative Hospital Service Organizations

501(f): Cooperative Service Organizations of Operating Educational Organizations

501(k): Publicly Available Childcare Organizations

501(n): Charitable Risk Pools

How did COVID-19 affect grant funding?

What happened during the pandemic for small businesses and nonprofits when it came to grants?

Once the pandemic hit, suddenly, everybody wanted to help. We made it a challenge for everyone who was working for GrantWatch to locate a grant that would help with COVID recovery. And that's what happened. It was just such a great feeling for my staff to be able to put in this extra work. The corporations, foundations, and government agencies were also coming through.

And what we found then were about 1,500 grants from corporations, foundations, government agencies. Many corporations stepped into the void and said, "We want to help."

With that many COVID related grants available, GrantWatch needed to create a separate Coronavirus COVID-19 category. The category filled up very quickly. As I put the finishing touches on my book in December 2023, there were still 153 Coronavirus COVID-19 grants available.

How are federal grants scored?

With the federal government, the grants are scored objectively, with points and values for each section. Federal agencies may hire grant readers or peer reviewers. For some grant applications, the review may be done in-house and that is an agency decision. However, for grant offerings involving multiple awards and where many applications are expected, they contract hire.

When you apply for a federal grant, there are questions in each section and corresponding points and often there'll be extra preference or bonus points. For example, if your organization serves a minority community or you are located in an enterprise zone, different items will add extra points. You need to submit the documentation to prove you qualify.

As you review your draft application, do your own evaluation, and ask yourself if you deserve the full point value for each section. If not, add to it, beef it up and most of all make sure you have fully answered the question. Every missed opportunity lowers your score.

When a grant is being scored the reviewer has a list of items to check off and the inclusion or absence of which is your score. The grant reviewer enters a summary score for each section based on the items list. If you have fully responded to the question, you will get the entire score allotment.

Reread the application carefully and identify where you might lose points. I cannot emphasize enough the magnitude of staying on top of points.

Here's an example question: "Describe the target population for the proposed program and your outreach efforts to obtain that goal." (15 points)

Let's say you mostly answer the question. You're opening a preschool, and you thoroughly discuss the targeted cross-section of the community it will serve. In addition, let's say you add a local newspaper advertisement for the preschool opening. It sounds like a wonderful project, however, there are holes in your narrative.

The reviewer may write that while you fully described the target population, the applicant failed to describe a coordinated effort to achieve that goal. Only a local newspaper advertisement for the preschool opening was mentioned, but nothing about the logistics of how you will achieve your goals.

And with that, you receive 13 points rather than 15. Two points just became the deciding factor in whether your organization will receive the funding you need. If you don't pay close attention to detail and don't fully answer questions, you will not make the cut for a highly competitive grant.

How are foundation grants scored?

Every foundation operates differently. As a general rule, most foundation grant applications will be screened for completeness by staff. The foundation prioritizes applications that are in line with their mission and vision.

Applications that meet all the requirements and are in line with the foundation's goals will be further screened by a committee of the board for content, plausibility, sustainability, replicability, and future dissemination of the model program.

The recommended set of viable applications will be read by the full board and decisions will be made based upon the ask amounts and available funding.

Why should we apply for a particular grant?

A few questions to ask yourself and your organization:

- Why do we want to win this grant?

- How will it help the audience we serve?

- How will it grow our organization?

- Does it fit with the mission of our organization?

- How do I win this grant?

When will I be notified if I win a grant?

Once you've submitted your grant proposal, the waiting game begins. The amount of time it takes to receive a grant approval varies depending on the funding source. Generally, foundations have their own timeline for reviewing proposals, and the time from submission to notification can range anywhere from a week to a year or longer.

On the other hand, federal and state government funding usually list their processing times publicly on their website.

Notifications may come through the US Post Office or FedEx or the like to avoid scams, or it may come through email.

The funding source will not request any money from you or any advance taxes to be paid. Remember, as stated previously, if you did not apply for a grant and you receive a notification that you won a grant – it is not real, (even though you wish it was). Scammers never give up trying to get your information and your money.

When you applied for the grant, the documents or website may have provided some information of notice. Otherwise, in your communication with the funder, you may want to ask the question about an estimate of time when you would receive notification and how that notification will arrive. If it is email, check your spam as it may be from an email address your provider is not used to.

Mark your grants calendar, which can be found under "My Account" on GrantWatch, and also make note in your personal planner of when to start looking for the notification.

When applying, be sure to use an email address that you and your organization have access to. If a consultant grant writer is submitting the grant for you or your organization, have them use an organization email address and at some later point when the grant writer is no longer working on a project, the organization can change the password, on the account.

A grant should never be viewed as the only thing to save an organization. The grant writer has no control over the decision for the funding of a grant, or the time of notice. If you hire a grant writer, you need to be part of the writing process by reviewing the grant for completeness of each deliverable service, completed by the grant writer.

Is it easier to apply for a foundation grant than a government grant?

Private foundations are a popular source of funding for a wide range of projects. The application process for foundation grants can be less complicated than federal grants.

Foundations usually have scheduled meetings and notice of when they will send out award letters. While board members may or may not vote for grant winners, the bureaucracy is less complicated.

The application process for federal grants and other government grants can be more complicated and time-consuming than applying for private foundation grants. You may find the notification dates under the application deadline. The potential funding amount for government grants is generally more significant.

Federal grants and other state, city, and local grants can have specific scoring guidelines. For example, many have stipulations regarding font size, margins, number of pages, and character counts.

What is the likelihood of your proposal being funded?

It's worth noting that the chance of receiving a grant depends on the number of applicants, the amount of money available, alignment with the funding organization's priorities and the quality of your proposal.

To increase the chances of a proposal being funded, it is important to thoroughly research the funding organization, understand their objectives and criteria, and tailor the proposal accordingly. The proposal should be well written. It should clearly articulate the need for the project, demonstrate the potential impact and feasibility of the proposed activities, provide a detailed budget, and include a strong evaluation plan.

Whenever possible, engage in effective communication with the funding source and address any questions or concerns they may have. Submit the proposal before the deadline to maximize the chances of funding.

Collaborate with relevant stakeholders, demonstrate community support, and highlight your organization's capacity and track record to enhance the likelihood of funding.

The decision to fund a proposal rests with the funding source.

How can I maximize our chances of success?

To increase your odds of success, it's advisable to apply for multiple grants and not rely solely on one source of revenue.

While the time it takes to receive grant approval can vary, new grants become available each day. Keep checking grant databases regularly to stay updated on the latest funding opportunities.

What are my options if my grant proposal is rejected?

Take it as an opportunity to learn and improve. Spend time reviewing your application to ensure that you followed all guidelines and didn't make any mistakes.

Ask for feedback by calling the foundation or government agency and speaking with a program officer. Be gracious and thank them for their time and consideration. Building a relationship with the foundation or government agency will be helpful for future applications.

If you're new to the grants game, and after submitting your first grant you realize that completing future grant applications is not in your wheelhouse, you should then consider hiring a grant writer to help improve your future chances of success.

What do I do with my rejected grant proposal?

Your rejected grant proposal may still be a great piece of writing. Don't discard it! You have spent a lot of time gathering information and documents that support your application.

You might want to preserve your application and apply again in the next grant cycle. If you can obtain the reviewers' notes, you can also use them as a guide to improve your application to gain more points in the next cycle.

Many of the sections of your application can be improved, tweaked, and retrofitted to become part of a different grant application.

As a grant writer you will want to save everything you have written for future applications.

How can I obtain reviewers' notes and scores given to my application?

If you have submitted a federal grant proposal and are interested in obtaining the reviewers' notes and scores, you can make a request through the federal agency or the Freedom of Information Act (FOIA).

To request your grant review, you will need to follow the agency's specific instructions to obtain this information. Typically, this involves writing a formal request letter or filling out a request form, providing your grant proposal number and other identifying information, and paying any associated fees.

Once you have received your grant review, take the time to carefully review the feedback and use it to strengthen your proposal for future grant opportunities.

What is an LOI, letter of intent?

Not all grants require a letter of intent or letter of inquiry. However, when they do, if you miss this step, you will not be able to apply.

Some foundations ask for an LOI before requesting a full grant proposal. A letter of Inquiry (LOI) is often also required for grant applications where unsolicited proposals are not accepted. The funder then reviews it before inviting the grant seeker to submit a full grant application.

GrantWatch does not publish grants that say, unsolicited proposals are not accepted and there is no request for an LOI.

If the LOI is approved, the applicant may then be invited to submit a full grant proposal. A funding source uses an LOI to determine if an applicant or a project aligns with their mission and funding priorities.

An LOI should be thought of as a mini-grant proposal where you will want to hit each of the points generally required in a full proposal. It is your one or two-page synopsis or elevator pitch. In the letter of intent, you will include the name and brief description of your organization, a summary of the proposed project, the amount of funding you are seeking, and how the project aligns with the funder's mission and priorities. Depending on the space allotment, you can include a brief overview of the needs, goals, objectives, activities, evaluation, and budget. Your organization's contact information should be checked and rechecked for accuracy.

Asking for an LOI can help the funder weed out organizations that are not a good fit or appropriate to receive their offered grant. Additionally, organizations also use the LOI to assess how much staff is needed to review the upcoming proposals.

An LOI has another benefit when required, because it allows organizations to gauge the interest of the funder and determine if it is worth the time and effort to submit a full proposal.

Additionally, it can also be a conduit for feedback from the funder so you can adjust and modify your proposed project before submitting a full application.

Overall, a letter of intent is a useful tool for nonprofits to use when seeking funding for their projects.

What range of monetary grants are available?

Every day, new grants become available. The challenge lies in determining the potential grant amount, which could vary widely. GrantWatch provides information on the dollar range for each listed grant when it's available. Some grants may be in-kind support, where services and/or goods are offered instead of monetary funds.

The range of grant awards is very broad, from $500 to even more than $5 million. The amount of funding depends on the applicant and the generosity of the funding source.

Federal government grants are typically substantial and can be hundreds of thousands or even millions of dollars. The amount is contingent on the government allocation and the specific purpose of the grant.

When you explore foundation grants on GrantWatch, you'll find links to the funding sources. You remember the 990 reports? This is the perfect time to utilize this tool. This research is crucial to understanding the typical grant sizes awarded.

For example: If a grant mentions a range of $1,000 to $10,000, and a closer look at their 990s and the funder's website reveals that the majority of past recipients received $10,000, you will then apply for $10,000.

With this knowledge, applicants can make informed decisions about the amount they request. Due diligence is essential to avoid counterproductive requests and increase the likelihood of securing meaningful funding.

How many grants can companies apply for at the same time?

If your company meets eligibility standards and it's not the same funder, you can apply for as many grants as you'd like. However, if you are lucky enough to get more than one grant awarded for the same program, you will need to advise the funding source, modify the budgets, and expand the program to serve more people.

The goal is to complete one application to perfection, before starting another.

How much does it cost to be a GrantWatch subscriber?

The goal of GrantWatch has always been to level the playing field for large and small organizations. We have held steady with our pricing over the years.

The best and most economical subscription is the $199, for the annual subscription. GrantWatch also offers both multiple-user packages and library licenses.

GrantWatch is a living, breathing search engine with many new grants added daily. Time expired grants are archived, and grant information is updated as we are notified.

The other high-value plan is the one that is quarterly for $90. This plan is excellent for start-ups, individuals, and nonprofits with specific funding needs and who have a good grasp of the grant writing process.

The $45 monthly and the $18 weekly subscriptions I typically recommend for beginners. If you're new to grant research and grant writing, a smaller plan is best while you get a feel for the work. It's also an excellent way to see the value of all the plans.

Quite honestly, I'm proud that we have been able to maintain our pricing. We have not reacted with the economy. In fact, the real beauty is that you can turn off your auto-renew feature independently and then choose a different pricing plan as needed. They are interchangeable and utterly self-managed. You have all the power to make the change yourself, at any time within the system.

Do private foundations receive grants?

In most cases, no. Recently, we received a call from a GrantWatch subscriber asking why their 501(c)3 private foundation is repeatedly denied when applying for grants.

Typically, private foundations do not receive grants. Upon investigation, we found that of the 276,227 funding sources on GrantWatch between 2015 and 2023 that have awarded grants, only 15,029 had awarded grants to private foundations, and most of those funders, themselves were private foundations. Grants are primarily awarded to 501(c)3 public charities.

Private foundations are established by individuals, families, or corporations and derive their financial resources from endowments, donors, investments, and contributions from their founders. For private foundations still interested in applying for grants, a list of funders who have granted to private foundations in the past, is available under the 990s tab on the navigation bar.

III: How To Write a Grant?

Now that you know how it all began for me, and have had your questions about grants answered, it is time to get down to the business of writing grants.

For some, this section will be a refresher course and a way to organize your skills. And for the novice, it will be your first foray into guided grant writing.

AI (artificial intelligence) grammar checks and spell checks are perfect when used sparingly. Do not use it as your content. And do not accept every change.

AI will not write with your passion and dedication and will provide you with many versions of a word salad that lacks your voice and dedication to your cause.

In fact, in my experience it will only confuse. You need to do the hard work of program development that matches the mission of the funding source and your organization. You need to complete your budget, the data of the needs of your organization, the goals and objectives, and the content for your responses.

Throughout my book I have suggested you write your first grant. After all, I wrote my first grant, and won. I know you can win, too. This may be the start of your next career. The only way to learn how to write a grant is to write one.

Please, feel free to use this section as a reference manual. It can work as your how-to guide to fill in the blank pages of a grant application.

Prepare to explore sections that speak about eligibility, following directions, passion, maps, and folders.

I have also prepared an in-depth review of all parts of a grant with writing samples that should be combined with your persuasive writing skills, and your passion for your organization's programs, goals, and the people you serve.

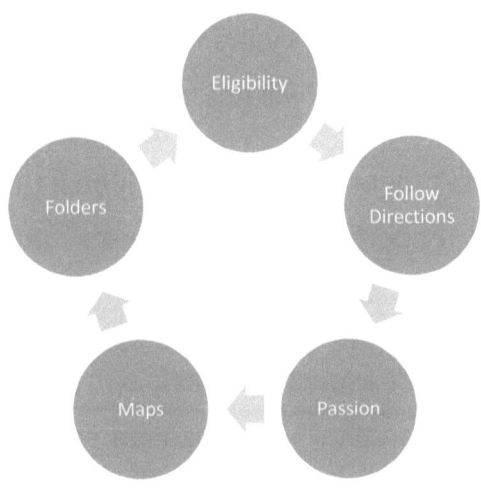

ELIGIBILITY

Are you eligible to apply for a grant? Before diving into the application process, it's crucial to always check the eligibility requirements. Applying for a grant you are not eligible for would be a waste of time and effort.

GrantWatch takes the grant jargon and translates it into simple everyday language. So, anyone can do a quick scan of the grant detail page and get the most important details immediately.

The initial step to applying for any grant is always assessing you or your organization's eligibility. Carefully review the eligibility requirements set by the funding source. And, just as important, read what they will not fund.

What if you don't meet the criteria? Is it best to move on and explore other opportunities? The quick answer is yes. However, you might also consider a change in perspective.

If there's a specific aspect you lack but can be fulfilled by partnering with another organization or through fiscal sponsorship, you might still consider pursuing the grant. Collaboration and forming coalitions can sometimes help bridge the eligibility gap.

However, you must watch the clock and keep in mind the time constraints of the application deadline. Decide if you have enough time to form a partnership and obtain a signed MOU, memorandum of understanding, with an organization that provides the missing component(s) listed in the eligibility criteria.

Another way to solve the problem is to write the component into the application as a subcontractor to provide that service. However, using a subcontractor may not speak to the experience and expertise of your organization. Explore the importance and the point value of the missing component in the application. This will help you determine which organization should take the lead as the applicant.

Let's say you're a nonprofit or a small business applying for a grant, and the RFP, request for proposals or grant documents, requires a component that you currently don't have and don't wish to provide.

For instance, if you're an after-school program and the funding criteria mentions the need for a parenting component, but you don't have one now, you can still strengthen your application. Identify a nonprofit down the road that has a successful parenting program, review the application with them, and create a memorandum of understanding to incorporate their expertise into your grant application. Think about how to word it in the application. For example: "In partnership with..." may sound a lot better.

If you have decided to apply for the grant, I wouldn't recommend that you approach an organization that meets all the criteria, because they can just apply themselves, without you.

What should you do if there's a component you simply cannot fulfill, such as a requirement for a five-year business existence when you've only been operating for six months? Do not assume that the grant committee will make an exception. Instead, you can write to the funding source and inquire. If you receive a positive response, then proceed with the application. Otherwise, move on. There will be other grants.

Writing a grant is a tedious process that involves a lot of cooperation within the organization.

Make your choice as to whether to apply, wisely. Ask yourself and your organization some key questions:

- Do we meet all the eligibility requirements?

- What is missing, and can we collaborate with another organization or business to fulfill those requirements?

- Are we an excellent fit or just passable?

- Review the funding source's grant awarding history to identify organizations with similar missions and gauge compatibility.

- Do we have enough time to meet the deadline?

- Have we missed any mandatory conferences?

- Have we missed a deadline for a mandatory LOI or any other pre-application requirements?

When my team at GrantWatch created the grant detail page, we aimed to make it user-friendly and easily shareable for board meetings or discussions. The page has undergone many revisions over the years to provide you with clear eligibility criteria.

The grant detail pages have enough information there for someone to use it in a presentation. It's certainly enough for a board to decide whether they should move forward and look through the complete application.

Imagine sitting around a large table during a weekly or monthly meeting, where you can print out a single page and make multiple copies for everyone to review. This highly organized page serves as a presentation tool, providing enough information for someone to present it and for the board to make an informed decision on whether to initially pursue the grant, upon further examination of the complete application.

The grant detail page contains all general eligibility criteria. However, it should never take the place of an in-depth review of the eligibility criteria within the full application packet.

Review a funder's 990 to determine your likelihood of getting funded.

Once you have established that you meet all the eligibility requirements, it is time to see who this funder has awarded in the past. It is important to understand and learn a little bit more about the funding source before you apply.

You increase your chances of getting funded when you apply to grants offered by funders who are the best fit for your organization. The information provided on the funder's IRS 990 report may give you a better idea of the likelihood of your organization being funded.

The 990s can tell you a few things, most of all who and for what purposes they have funded organizations in the past. Think about it logically. If your organization has similarities to a previously funded organization, it's in your best interest to apply for a grant from the same funder.

The amounts of previous grant awards will give you a ballpark figure of how much money they generally award in individual grants. On the GrantWatch detail page and on the actual RFP of the funding source you will see a range or an exact amount of the grant. The 990 report will also help you decide how much to apply for in funding.

GrantWatch displays the amount of money remaining in their foundation at the end of the tax year. This may also help you decide. If the grant lists how many organizations they plan to fund, you can do some calculations by dividing that number into 5% of the dollar amount in their foundation. There are some IRS calculations of how much they need to distribute per year. Review this with your CPA to make an educated decision.

Look at the previous years of the 990s to determine if they spend most funds to compensate the board and leadership, before you think a large amount of money is available for grant awards.

The 990s will tell you who is on their Board, their titles, and their time commitment. If you dig deeper into the raw data of the 990s from previous years, you will see the individual amount of compensation for each board member. On GrantWatch, we show the name, title, and time commitment.

Perhaps you have a connection to someone and wish to contact them and give them your elevator pitch. Lobbying is not prohibitive for foundations, but it is with government agencies.

On the grant detail page, GrantWatch now has links to the 990s of the funding sources, when available.

When fiscal sponsorship is needed.

If the eligibility of a grant is for a nonprofit, you will need to be a nonprofit, or obtain a fiscal sponsor.

If your organization already has an IRS letter of final determination, please skip this section and go to section called "Following Directions."

I used to hear from prospective grant writing clients, who were small businesses, "We are a nonprofit because we do not make any profit. Why can't we apply?" Sorry, that is not what meets the eligibility criteria of nonprofit status.

There is also a marked difference between a local nonprofit that has nonprofit status from their state and a 501(c)(3) IRS nonprofit that has received a letter of determination giving them nonprofit status as a public charity.

Most of the time when grant eligibility is nonprofit, you are required to have a final letter of determination from the IRS saying that you are a 501(c)(3) nonprofit.

When applying for a state grant, the state might accept your nonprofit status, because they gave it to you.

But in general, you need more. When a nonprofit decides a grant is for them, but they don't already have the nonprofit status, they won't have time to apply and receive approval. It takes six to eight months and sometimes longer to obtain nonprofit status.

A small nonprofit may not even have the funds to pay someone to file for their nonprofit status. That's where a fiscal sponsor may come in.

I am including text from an exceedingly popular blog article, on GrantNews from GrantWatch: "Organizations Can Apply for Grants and Donations Prior to 501(c)(3) Tax-Exempt Status Through a Fiscal Sponsor." This article demystifies fiscal sponsorship.

According to the National Network of Fiscal Sponsors (NNFS), fiscal sponsorship has evolved as an effective and efficient method of applying for grants, starting new nonprofits, seeding social movements, and delivering public services.

Fiscal sponsorship refers to a legal arrangement in which a nonprofit organization agrees to accept and administer funds for another entity with a parallel mission. That entity can be another nonprofit, but often doesn't yet have the legal tax-exempt status. By partnering with a fiscal sponsor, a charitable project can seek and receive tax-exempt contributions right away without having to establish a new independent organizational infrastructure or apply for 501(c)(3) status. The fiscal sponsor provides fiduciary services including governance, funds management and other necessary administrative support to projects with social impact missions in alignment with their own.

Any nonprofit agency deemed an exempt public charity by the IRS can be a fiscal sponsor for a nonexempt community project. The fiscal sponsor must have been awarded its tax-exempt status under Section 501(c)(3) of the Internal Revenue Code and have a legally binding agreement with the project. With that agreement, charitable contributions are given to the fiscal sponsor, which then grants them to support the cause. Being able to claim these contributions as tax-deductions encourages potential donors to support these valuable community projects.

Fiscal sponsors "have the ability to receive charitable contributions for specific projects, the infrastructure to ensure compliance with applicable federal and state laws and adequate internal controls to ensure that the funds will be used for the intended charitable purposes," according to a recent IRS report. Only nonprofits whose executive leadership and boards of directors are fully aware of the obligations and liabilities they legally assume should agree to be fiscal sponsors.

Fiscal sponsors can be found by searching on Google for the *Fiscal Sponsorship Directory*. There are a number of organizations that have created lists and networks.

Fiscal sponsors generally charge an administrative fee based on a percentage of the budget of the sponsored organization or program. These fees can range based on the services that are provided and the complexity of grants to be administered.

According to attorney Gregory L. Colvin in his transformational book, *Fiscal Sponsorship: 6 Ways to Do It Right*, there are several models of fiscal sponsorship.

Fiscal sponsorship can be practiced under various models approved by the IRS. The two most-frequently used models are comprehensive fiscal sponsorship and pre-approved grant relationship fiscal sponsorship.

Comprehensive Fiscal Sponsorship is an inclusive financial support relationship whereby the fiscally sponsored project becomes a program of the fiscal sponsor. The fiscal sponsor maintains all legal and fiduciary responsibility for the sponsored project, including its employees and activities. This model of fiscal sponsorship is particularly valuable when a project has employees.

The Pre-Approved Grant Relationship Fiscal Sponsorship is a fiscally sponsored project that does not become a program belonging to the sponsor but is a separate entity responsible for managing its own tax reporting and liability issues. In addition, the sponsor does not necessarily maintain ownership of any part of the results of the project's work— ownership rights may be addressed in the fiscal sponsor agreement and could potentially result in some form of joint ownership. The sponsor simply assures that the project will use the grant funds received to accomplish the ends described in the grant proposal. This is the model of fiscal sponsorship primarily used in the arts.

Using a fiscal sponsor satisfies IRS requirements as long as the fiscal sponsor maintains the right to decide how it will use contributions. Programs seeking sponsorship should be aware of this and be sure that the fiscal sponsor they choose is truly solid and, in a position, to take them on.

Since most funding sources give to organizations, not individuals, fiscal sponsorship may help you qualify for more funding opportunities, enabling you to fund and start your project sooner.

Please take all necessary precautions because there have been cases where fiscal sponsors have gone into deficit or have even gone bankrupt, bringing the projects down with them. Make sure that fiscal sponsors have insurance in place to ensure that they are able to pay the funds due for the projects they sponsor, should they become fiscally unstable.

Fiscal sponsorships allow programs to be eligible for foundation grants and other grants they need.

Follow Directions

Successful grant writing often comes down to common sense. Once you have established eligibility, the next step is to carefully read the directions. Make a list for yourself of formatting directions.

If a funding source provides the applicant with directions, common sense says that they should be carefully followed. Every proposed program has a lot of moving parts, but the grant application itself needs to follow a unique set of instructions.

There is an expectation in the grant world that an organization applying for a grant, if funded, will appropriately manage grant funds. Demonstrating your ability to follow written directions gives the funder confidence in your organization.

When the grant reviewer scores your application, they generally have a checklist of bullet points to check for each section which they will then tally to provide your overall score.

If your response is in the wrong section, prepare to lose points.

Recently, I interviewed a foundation that was the exception to the rule. They were much more lenient than I had expected about following directions. However, upon further examination, I realized that their grant applications were for small grants. They were looking for a creative use of a small amount of money that would align with their mission.

If directions are not followed, it generally leads to disqualification from a government agency or large foundation. Grant reviewers will typically weed out the applications that did not follow the instructions, to the letter.

What does it mean to follow ALL directions?

Pay attention to format.
- type of font
- font size
- line spacing
- margins
- character or word count/limit
- page limits

- Restate the question or prompt in your answer.
    - address each bullet point.
    - demonstrate you have met all requirements.

- Meet deadlines.
  - LOI
  - Q & A question and answers submission
  - Conference attendance
  - Grant deadline

Each grant has its own unique application process. Some foundations utilize a standardized application form. Other applications are fully online with a character count for each space allotted. Other online applications have you upload a fully formatted document with excel budget forms. The directions may even include something as minute as how to name the file you are uploading.

Pay attention. Do not lose points over minutia or lose an opportunity to have your application read because of not following directions.

When grant writing, I always take the question and turn it into the beginning of my answer. Let's say you asked me a question. Now, in the beginning of my paragraph, I'm going to write that I'm answering your question. That's going to be the beginning of my paragraph. And I'm going to make sure that I hit every little point.

If there are space constraints, then I take their question and make it my brief heading. If there are parts to a question, I would use subheadings.

This is a process that works for me and helps me manage all those minute details that could mean the loss of a point. And who knows, maybe that one point is the difference between winning a grant and not getting the funding.

Now, let's touch on conferences. If there is a mandatory conference, and the date has passed, don't apply. If the conference is not mandatory, and you can listen to the conference recording or view the webinar or even obtain a list of questions asked and answered, then go ahead, and apply.

Federal grant formatting guidelines.

If you exceed the page limits in a federal grant application, your application may be rejected or disqualified from consideration. The federal agencies that award grants typically have strict guidelines and requirements for grant applications, including page limits, font size, and margins.

These guidelines are designed to ensure fairness and consistency in the review process and to make it easier for reviewers to assess and compare applications. With the federal government, if they tell you to use 12-point font and you don't, they're not reading your application.

If they tell you to single space, do not double space. If you submit a grant application that exceeds the page limits, it may be returned to you without review or even be disqualified from consideration altogether.

In some cases, the agency may provide instructions for how to modify the application to meet the guidelines and resubmit it, but this is not always the case.

It is important to carefully review the guidelines for each grant application and adhere to the specified page limits and formatting requirements to increase your chances of success in obtaining federal grant funding.

Here is a mistake to learn from: I once left a grant application that included detailed specific formatting requirements with a grant writer, I trusted to submit for me. I was going on vacation, and they submitted it after completing the final minor edits.

I didn't have a minute to spare, or I would have missed my flight. After working for 4 weeks, day and night on a grant application, my bags were packed, and I had to go.

The person that submitted the grant was also in pre-vacation mode and was editing too close to the deadline. When the grant was submitted it was not formatted into single space and also did not follow the directions of font size, margin, and page limits.

We had an excellent budget in the application and a great budget narrative. However, no one got to read it. The grant exceeded the page limit.

We didn't get that grant. In the reviewers' notes it said, "The applicant exceeds the 60-page limit due to font size and formatting issues (single spacing). Therefore, no detailed budget information was included. (No page found)

> **Criterion 4: Budget and Budget Justification (15 points)**
>
> *Strengths:*
> No strengths noted.
>
> *Weaknesses:*
> — The applicant exceeds the 60 page limit due to font size and formatting issues (single spacing). Therefore, no detailed budget information was included. (No page found)

The one good thing to come out of losing that grant is the lesson I can now pass on to you. Learn from my mistakes! Following directions is key to winning a grant and if you want to win a grant, you must be present for all aspects of the application process through to submission.

PMF: Passion, Maps and Folders

I created the mnemonic, PMF, to help me explain to others how to write a grant.

Passion is your enthusiasm, your devotion, and your team's energy. It needs to jump off the page. Passion will set your application apart from all the others.

Maps show how you build and develop your program from goals through to the budget. It is an alignment of all parts of a grant. What are the needs? What are the goals? What are the objectives? What activities will you perform to meet those objectives? And how will you evaluate those objectives? What needs to be in your budget to accomplish all your programmatic goals?

Folders are every license, document, resume, IRS letter of determination, and corporate papers. These folders house all the stats, newspaper articles, research, and everything that shows that the need really exists. You need these items at your fingertips to be grant-ready.

Why did I create the mnemonic, PMF?

It was 2020 and I was in public speaking training with Hey, Sandy! PR & Communications. I was a bit rusty from my 2001 run for City Council. They had booked me on a few TV and podcast spots and Sandy in her thoroughness wanted to make sure I was ready. I was freezing up and was unable to gather my thoughts, even though this was something I could usually teach in my sleep.

Sandy said, "Libby, you can do this! Girl, you got this! Do it again!" And she was right! But I couldn't get my thoughts organized quickly enough for live TV.

I am a thinker first. That is kind of why my friends don't like to play Mahjong with me. I think, and then sometimes I win – but it slows down what is a fast game. Then I hear that faint whisper, "Oh she's very competitive." Which I am!

I tried sticky notes but didn't want to end up reading from them. I did not need to read, I needed to speak about my passion.

I created the mnemonic PMF and now, that's all I need to remember. Everything flows easily from there. I hope it works for you, too.

Let's review: To write a grant for an organization, think eligibility, follow directions, and PMF (passion, maps and folders).

Passion

Why are you doing all of this? Grant writing is an all-encompassing endeavor. Why are you writing a grant?

Pain gives you passion. What's your pain point? And believe me, when somebody is writing a grant, they're dealing with pain.

The reader needs to be able to feel your pain. When you write, you need to make the reader feel your pain and the passion for your cause.

If two grants were of equal value, what makes a funder choose one over the other? The answer is that the reader - or funder - has connected with your cause (sharing that pain point) for positive human impact.

Think back to my first grant written to the Tandy Corporation. Why was I successful? Why did a rookie win one of only four Tandy-funded grants across the country? Because I was passionate about wanting my special education students to learn to read and my passion jumped off the page. What was my pain point? The upcoming state writing test, my need to motivate my students to write, and teaching them to accept edits and correct their own work.

When writing, keep in mind why you are in the nonprofit sector. In addition, stop and consider whether you can make a believer out of your reader.

It starts within your organization. You need to develop a team of people who feel the pain point and share your passion. Once you have a solid team in place, it's time to develop those important connections outside your organization.

Passion, Partnerships and Consortiums

Does your organization have enough experience in all components of the application to achieve the full points if you go it alone? Will another organization or a coalition bring more passion? Will their energy, expertise and experience enhance your organization? Will they give you access to a wider target population?

Keep in mind that if a partner can do what your organization can't do, then their history becomes your cumulative history within the application.

The reader will see the strength of the two organizations together, with one being a complement to the other, each bringing their own valuable expertise to the table.

Pitch your program to find people within the community who are excited and passionate about your proposed program. You want to find people who want to participate with either a letter of support, or in a partnership, or in a consortium. When you develop partnerships, you tap into untapped resources. Search through your contacts, do some networking, make some phone calls, and schedule a meeting or site visit.

When asking an organization or a community leader for a letter of support, I would always draft a few versions of a sample letter. The letter would explain how that person or organization knew my organization and it would include the title of the grant application and the title of the program. My letter would also include the overall goals and any in-kind support that was agreed upon.

When developing a memorandum of understanding for a partnership, I would draft it to clearly outline the resources each partner will contribute to the project, such as staff time, in-kind contributions, delivery of services, or offering training or expertise.

My passion and that of many others, was the driving force and success of these two grant applications that were funded over and over again for multiple years. The HHS Youth Gang Drug Prevention Program was initially funded for $360,000 and the first year of Staten Island's Child Health Plus, NYS DOH was funded for $700,000.

Maps

You must stay hyper-focused. What's the plan? You need to map it out. There are many moving parts within a grant, and just like this book, they must clearly relate to each other. The connection must be clear.

Your map is the full blueprint for your grant. The map takes everything into account from beginning to end.

Let's look at the overall map. What you will do when developing a new grant proposal is create your own planner, spreadsheet, post-it notes, or workflow document to illustrate your map. We all use different tools, so I want you to let it flow into your own dynamic method of working.

Before you begin, go back to the grant application, and re-examine the funder's mission and what programs they will and will not fund. Also, review the target audience written about on their website and in their grant documents.

We begin with the pain; in grant terms it is called the needs that motivate your passion. You have goals to solve the pain. Objectives to achieve the goals and to meet the needs. Activities are the actions that everyone will be involved in to achieve each objective. Evaluation will include pre, post and midpoint evaluations, along with summative and formative reports, to evaluate if the objectives have been met in the attainment of your goals.

You will diagram a table of organization that maps out the staffing and/or consultants for the activities, evaluation, and funds management. Also, you will calculate a budget that considers everything you need to purchase and the people to hire to achieve your goals and objectives and evaluate your program.

When you write a grant, you need to stay focused and thoroughly map it out. If you describe a need, then your goal should fill that need. If you're writing about a need, and then you present a program that doesn't relate to the need, there's no matchup. Why did you mention that need in your grant?

I want to set the stage: A capable 11-year-old child, on school vacation, asks their parent, "I would like to get an allowance." And in the child's next sentence they ask, "Are we going to the Animatron Museum today?"

There's no follow through; it's a disjointed thought. The entire request can be forgotten.

But what if the conversation went very differently? "Mom, I just turned 11 and I would like to get an allowance. I am a good kid, you said so yourself, and I want to save for my own laptop to make my drawings of comic book heroes come alive. I want them to walk and talk."

In this example, the child stayed on track. The reason for the allowance is qualified, and the parent will most probably be on board.

What's the plan? When you write a grant, you need to stay focused and map it out. The program narrative must have continuity and remain focused on the outcomes aligned with your mission and that of the funding source:

- Needs

- Goals – long range goals

- Measurable Objectives

- Activities – Action Plan – step by step

- Staffing

- Timelines

- Evaluation that measures attainment of the goals and objectives

- Budget – every item in the budget MUST be mentioned in the narrative.

Now when I think about a project, I think in terms of needs, goals, objectives, activities, timeline, and evaluation. I personally start with a spreadsheet.

I break it up so that every need has a goal. Every goal has its objectives, and every objective has activities designed to achieve those objectives. And all along I have been thinking how I can measure the attainment of each objective. I make a shopping list on the side of all my new budgetary needs and what resources we already have that can be used for the program.

Your elevator pitch.

You are at the office of a foundation. The person you planned to meet with was running late and now they are only giving you four minutes of their time.

"Walk with me," you are told.

This is it – time for your elevator pitch.

Can you explain why the foundation should fund your program? (Alignment with their mission)

Can you explain what sets your organization apart from everyone else vying for the same funds? (Organizational Capacity)

Can you describe the need within your target audience and your overall goals? (Needs and Goals)

Can you explain why your organization is most capable of solving the need? (Organizational Capacity)

Can you explain your brilliantly innovative program that will diminish the need? (Activities)

Can you describe the actual deliverables and within what timeframe? (Objectives)

Can you quickly account for the dollar amount needed and on what most of the money will be spent? (Budget)

Can you explain how you will know if you attained your goals? (Evaluation)

Practice answering these questions. Then sit down to write a very convincing LOI, if requested and if not start mapping your full grant application.

Writing an LOI.

When an LOI is required or suggested, you should write one. Read the funder's written directions, follow them carefully, and meet the deadline. Your LOI needs to demonstrate your passion and should be a brief one or two-page document.

The specific requirements of an LOI may vary depending on the preferences of the funding source.

I have seen where an LOI is a list of difficult questions that will require research within your organization, and I have seen a short qualifying quiz on the Internet. Other times I have seen a two pager with character count for each section.

An LOI can be more difficult to write than a full grant proposal because of the limitations of space. Foundations usually provide an outline for their requested LOI.

In general, an LOI without specific written instructions should be addressed to a specific contact person at the foundation receiving the LOIs.

Include the following, in a brief, 2-page passionate and informative letter that summarizes your ultimate full proposal.

Use the official organization letterhead. The letterhead should include the contact person at your agency.

Address the letter to the funding source's contact person, and then underneath write the legal name of the funding source and the organization's address.

The opening of your LOI needs to be one of those "gotcha" moments. It should be an engaging, concise executive summary (name of your organization, organization's history, experience, and expertise) that inspires the reader to continue.

Include the name of the grant you are applying for, the title of your project and/or why you are writing the LOI. Include the amount of money you are requesting, as well as a brief description of the project involved. You should also include how your project and organization fits the funder's guidelines and funding interests.

Statement of Need or Background: The needs section provides information about the organization's history, experience, and expertise. Make a connection between what you currently do within the community or population and what you want to accomplish with their funding. Show the need by mentioning statistical facts about the specific target population that clearly demonstrate the need for the grant.

Project Description: The project description outlines how you plan to use the funding to solve the problem in the needs statement. Describe the goals, objectives, and activities. It may also include a timeline and a budget. Include a mention of major activities, along with the names and titles of key project staff.

Expected Outcomes and Evaluation: The expected outcomes section describes the anticipated results of the project or program, and how it will benefit the target population. Explain briefly how you will evaluate the success of your program.

Organizational Capacity: The capacity section explains the organization's ability to carry out the proposed project, including its staff, resources, and partnerships. Include any funding already secured toward this program and how you plan to support the project in the future.

Conclusion: The conclusion summarizes the main points of the LOI and includes a thank you statement of appreciation for the funder's consideration. Sign the LOI, with a business salutation such as "Sincerely."

If there was a guidance provided by the funding source for the LOI, read it over one more time before submitting. The LOI, when required, is a mini or pre-proposal and will get you in the door to submit a full proposal.

Needs

All the subscribers on GrantWatch have a definitive need for a grant. However, not everyone who writes a grant will get one. Hopefully, you will win the grants you write.

First, grants are not guaranteed. They are highly competitive. Second, how you write the grant within your organization makes all the difference.

The needs sections of grant proposals drive the goals, objectives, program activities and the evaluation objectives. The budget is the foundation of the grant application."

Having been a federal grant reviewer myself – I have seen first-hand when the proposed program will not meet the needs of the target population.

We can predict this when each grant section was written by a separate individual in an organization that obviously had little or no communication. And when it is obvious that there was definitely no mapping!

Before you begin a grant, ask yourself:

- Who is the grant recipient? an individual, a small business, or a nonprofit?

- Can you define the geographic boundaries, and the age, and description (size, ages, characteristics, challenges, and lack of opportunities) of your target audience?

Do you know your target audience's needs?

- What programs do you currently provide to meet those needs?

- What is on your programmatic wish list? Identify the purpose for which you require a grant.

Now, let's discuss the process of finding a grant that meets the needs of your target population. Consider how you begin searching for a grant. For example, if you're an artist planning a community project, you would search for grants in the arts and culture category.

It's beneficial to focus on grants with deadlines at least six weeks away or those with ongoing deadlines. Starting with micro-grants (under $10,000) or in-kind grants (goods or services) can help build a grant award history.

Suppose you're a small business aiming to train young people in the field of silversmithing, which is currently a rare skill. You may have a desire to pass on your knowledge and ensure the skill doesn't fade away over time.

In this case, you would explore opportunities for workforce training, possibly reaching out to post-secondary schools and proposing the addition of silversmithing to their art curriculum.

It's important to understand that a grant should serve a purpose beyond personal gain or avoiding work. Grants are intended to support projects or programs that contribute to the greater good.

Every foundation, every funding source, whether it be government, federal, state, city, local, or foundation or corporation, has a mission and a vision of what they want to fund, how they want to spend their money, and what's important to them.

Grants are awarded by these funding sources based on what they're interested in funding. There are grants for almost anything. You have to continuously look and be flexible and be able to compromise a little bit and spin your needs (honestly) according to the needs of the community that you're serving and what the funding source wants to fund.

What are the needs of your community (your target audience)? Does the needs of the community align with the needs your organization wants to solve and how?

The needs section demonstrates the need for the goals, objectives, and activities. You need to align the needs of your target audience, who you want to serve, with the funder's mission, and show that your program goals are to remediate the needs.

To establish the need, you want to find:

- Statistics and data that provide evidence of the need.
- Best practices - evidence-based research.
- Best practices - review of literature.
- Community issues to establish the need.
- Neighborhood maps.
- Quote studies and newspaper articles.

Goals

Do your homework. How will your goals connect to those of the grantor? Do your research on the 990s and look at the purposes and types of grants they have awarded in the past, as well as the companies who have been the recipients.

Whenever possible, reach out to their grants or investment director and ask about their goals, tell them about your project to see if your vision is in line with theirs.

Mostly, be a great listener! Do not talk yourself out of something by saying too much at first.

What do you hope to accomplish?

Do your goals meet the needs?

Turn each need that you describe into a goal.

Measurable objectives – outcomes

An objective is more specific than a goal. It defines how you will achieve a part or the entire goal. There can be a few objectives for one goal.

Objectives can be written with all the parts below or just as simple outcomes which identify the change, depending upon space and the guidance in the grant application.

An objective or outcome is a result of an activity or action that you will do to achieve the goal. The objective is to make a significant statistical change, identified as a percentage of improvement, or a significant qualifying number of improvements.

The objective defines who will benefit. The beneficiaries or specific group relates back to the needs of your target audience and as described in your goal.

Finally, it identifies over what period the change will happen and the method of evaluation to achieve the outcome. Often, we use pre- and post-testing comparisons to achieve a score of the change.

What activities will help you achieve your specific goal? And what evaluation tool will be used to compare the results of pre and post activities?

The "as measured by" in an objective, ties right into the evaluation. Here, in your objective, you get to hint at the pre and post testing and the accomplishment measurement of the objective. In the evaluation section of the grant, you can be more specific – and it follows and flows from there.

Activities

What activities will help you meet your goals and objectives? The activities section is where you explain your program. This is where you describe all the actions and activities you are planning to engage in, to accomplish your goals and objectives.

Here you have the chance for freer and more passionate writing to help emphasize the specific activities you are planning to accomplish each objective. There can be multiple activities for one objective.

I personally like to create a timeline for my activities before writing a description of the program.

Timelines

Your activities should follow a calendar and be organized sequentially. The first column of the timeline breaks down all activities, including hiring staff all the way to dissemination of the evaluation and possibly a thank you letter to the funding source.

The timeline is your map of all grant related activities throughout the funding period of the grant, leading to the attainment of the objectives. Some people call the activities section, process objectives.

The timeline is your map. It identifies the start and end dates. As you work on the first column and identify in which months things will happen, you will surely want to return to your objectives and change your timing.

I prefer to divide the chart into months, or number the months – when there is no knowledge as to the receipt of funding and start date. For space constraints, some people divide into quarters.

On the left-side column is the description of the activity. The second column is your person(s) responsible column. And you will have either 12 thin columns for months or four, for quarters.

For example: At the start of the search for a program director, there would be a checkbox in month one. Interview the final three candidates. That could be in month two.

There are a variety of timelines you can include in a grant, and templates are available all over the Internet. The Gantt Chart is a type of bar chart that illustrates a project schedule. This chart uses horizontal bars in the graph to show the duration of each activity. The chart can be a colorful depiction of activities.

You can also make your own timeline very easily in Word using the table feature. What you use depends upon the space allowed or whether the application provides or directs the template.

A grant timeline in your grant proposal outlines the scheduled start and end dates for activities, also known as process objectives:

The timeline should include all tasks or activities needed to implement the program.

The timeline should include all tasks, starting from the day funding is announced or awarded to the last day of the project's funding period.

The timeline should illustrate how each task is built on the previous task and completed within the proposed time frame.

The timeline should include evaluation activities.

And finally, the timeline should designate the person or persons responsible for the supervision, who will implement the activity, and the completion date of the activity.

Evaluation

How will you evaluate each program component?

What methods will you use to prove or demonstrate the success of your program? Did you accomplish your objectives? Did you meet your goal?

Outcome Assessment: Start evaluating before you start the program. The pre-test information is of utmost importance. You can use standardized tests. When the schedules of the tests and the program align, recently administered tests can be used as a pre-test and the next scheduled standardized test can either be a midpoint or a posttest assessment (if it is within the funding period).

If your goal was to increase participation in Parenting Education, you can use sign-in sheets of attendance at PTA meetings and sign-in sheets at midpoint and conclusion of the funding period. If your goal was increased knowledge and tools for parenting, you could use a questionnaire, pre and post, to evaluate if objectives have been met.

Summative Grant Evaluation: At the conclusion of the funding period, we do a summative evaluation, a review of the project's performance. We want to assess the grant's impact. Did the program achieve its intended outcomes and objectives?

When we measure the extent to which the project met its goals, we understand the overall success and we can also make some assumptions: The program may have areas that need improvement. The program is effective. We should repeat or expand the program the following year with a similar target audience.

We also ask the question, should the program be disseminated as a replicable model? Can we go back to the funding source and ask for additional funding to repeat the program? And can we use the evaluation to demonstrate success and seek new funding from other funding sources to sustain the program?

Did the program uncover additional needs that will help the target audience achieve greater success?

The final evaluation is sent to the funding source with a heartfelt thank you and a wish to continue engaging in the future.

Formative Grant Evaluation: Formative evaluation takes place during the grant-funded project. It assists with making necessary modifications, improving the program and adjustments. Sharing formative evaluation depends on the funding source's requirements.

It is a good idea to stay in touch and send work produced along the way. It makes for a lifeline for renewed funding and budget modifications much easier.

Formative evaluation helps to identify challenges, assesses the relevance of strategies, and makes timely adjustments to enhance the project's chances of success.

Formative evaluation is conducted with team meetings, surveys, and ongoing assessments.

While it may not be required to conduct both summative and formative evaluations, as humans we are always making judgements as to whether something is or is not working. In this way, we integrate a combination of evaluations throughout the program, ensuring that the summative evaluation will be an evidence-based account of the project's impact and outcomes.

Evaluation Consultant

While I was working in the Community School District's office, we included an evaluation consultancy as part of our federal grants budget. One company, well-acquainted with the district, would meet with the grant writers to plan the optimal evaluation strategy for the program.

We would collectively review the grant application, including its needs, goals, objectives, activities, and the funding source's request for a proposal. The evaluation consultant would then prepare a draft of the evaluation section of the grant application.

The grant writer would review and then modify the evaluation component before placing it into the grant.

Budget

The budget builds your application. Whether the grant is for a large amount or a small amount of money, make sure you clearly identify how the money will be spent and where the remainder of the funds will come from to complete the program.

When we speak about mapping, we are talking about continuity within an application.

When I am planning a meal for guests at my home, I have two pages. One is the menu of everything I want to cook and serve. Think of that as the outcome of a grant and the other is for the ingredients which will become my shopping list.

I then take my ingredients list to my pantry cabinets and my refrigerator (in-kind support budget). Here I can see what I have and cross it off my list, and finally, I am left with my shopping list (budget – funding request).

In-kind support can come from the applicant organization, from other sources within the community, or from other awarded grants.

Everything that you write about in your proposal that requires an item or a staff member or a consultant must have a source. If you are sending letters through regular mail, don't forget you need postage.

There should not be anything in your budget that is not written about in the previous sections. If you are missing a required item, before adding it to your budget, go back to the activity section and revise, so that you mention it in the program description activity section.

The budget must match the proposal. If, for example, you are requesting playground equipment in your budget, you should have been speaking about the use of the playground as an activity to meet the needs and achieve the desired outcome/objective.

If there's a need for a playground for children with disabilities in your community, then you need to mention how you will be purchasing playground equipment. In addition, cover how it will be modified for children with disabilities and how you are ordering specific equipment.

All the playground equipment should be itemized in the budget. Who is going to take care of the equipment? Who is going to handle security for the playground?

All of these questions come to mind as your grant is being reviewed. If this playground is for a school, the school will be maintaining the equipment and handling security. Now you have in-kind support for these necessary items in your budget.

If you are not itemizing and including model numbers for equipment, then the grant reviewer may be thinking, "I purchased a swing set for my own family; it cost a lot more than is being written here."

The reviewer is now doubting your budget because they know how much money they are offering, and they are thinking that even if they award the funds for this worthwhile program, the program will not be successful.

However, if you itemize and you show real costs and where the other funds are coming from, then your budget is believable.

A grant application is built upon the budget. Nothing will happen without funding. Ask yourself these questions:

- How much is allocated for the grant award?

- How much can you obtain from outside sources?

- How much can your organization provide as in-kind?

- How will I work it out?

When creating a budget, use Excel and create equations. If an item or a staff member is being used for only a short period of time during the week (and the rest of the time they are paid for with school funds), then show the full salary and the percentage of their salary and time to be paid for, from the grant.

And if that person is salaried by the school and they will not be paid additional funds, then you can show the percentage of time and salary as in-kind support. Funders love to see in-kind support from the organization and from outside sources.

It is important to limit the amount used for administration in your program. Funders want to see their money go to a worthy cause and not to be top heavy.

Another way to look at grants and budgets is as parts of a whole. If your organization is looking for a building to rent for a variety of programs, each grant-funded program (if the funder allows for rent) can be charged for a portion of the whole rent.

You can do the same thing with staffing. Think of a full-time person as a 1.0 FTE, and an employee that works only the equivalent of one eight-hour day per week as 0.2 FTE.

The FTE or full-time equivalent is the way employers calculate and reconcile employee hours. In the budget under personnel expenditures, use the % FTE and job titles of current staffing and new staff to be used for the program. Then break down that amount as to where the funding will come from: the % paid for from other sources, and the % of FTE being requested in the program budget.

In the grant application you will need all the job descriptions for titles listed in the budget. Additionally, for key staff that you know will be working in the program you will need their CVs, curriculum vitae. Quality CVs will demonstrate your capacity to implement the program.

There needs to be a narrative as to why each item requested in the budget is needed to accomplish the goals of the proposal. Are you seeking all the funding from one source or a few? Who will manage the funds? Can you demonstrate what makes your organization capable of managing large sums of money or government funding?

Keep in mind that a funding source likes to see the community is really involved in what you're doing. It shows that you are not just sitting in a room by yourself writing grants without input, deciding what is good for the community. Those programs fizzle out quickly. Programs with community stakeholders flourish and grow.

Besides your Excel budget or budget worksheet requested by the funding source, in most grants you need a budget narrative.

The budget narrative or budget justification explains in writing how every item in your budget is necessary to run a successful program.

Here is an example of a sentence in a budget narrative:

"Funds have been requested in the amount of $... for a swing set for children with disabilities, allowing for inclusion of the children in the physical exercise portion of the school day."

Table of organization

I generally like to include 2 tables of organization. One that shows the entire organizational staff and another that focuses on the proposed program.

The first will show the extent of the administrative oversight and responsibilities. It also shows where the program fits into the internal organizational structure of the organization or company.

The second table is the programmatic table of organization. It will clearly illustrate the proposed program's staffing plan. I have included some creative and colorful tables in the next chapter of this book. Get creative. The grant reviewers like creativity.

Management of grant funds

Prepare a boilerplate piece explaining fiscal management. There is usually a question about the process within your organization. Here is where you assure the funder that you have experience in fiscal management and organization protocols in place.

You can write about the experience of the CPA firm managing the funds of the organization and how checks are double signed. Include how you have a separate checking account for each grant, the annual budget of the organization, and the process for approval of expenditures.

And finally, expound on the amounts of grant funds that you have managed in the past, and speak about the audited financial report or any informal audits.

The funder must feel that your organization can be relied upon to manage grant funds appropriately.

Staffing

When it comes to staffing, you need to demonstrate the current agency administration, supervision, and management of all current programs.

You will also need the resumes of all existing staff members who will devote a portion of their time to the proposed program. Establish in the budget the portion of time to be devoted. Their resumes should demonstrate their ability, experience, and expertise in the role they will play in the grant-funded program.

The funding source also wants to see job descriptions for the TBAs (to be announced positions). What skills will be needed? And what percentage of time will be devoted to the program? Illustrate how the proposed program will be incorporated into the organization.

Staffing Chart

If a chart is required, every staff member and TBA position mentioned in the narrative and budget should appear on this chart as well as in the Table of Organization.

Folders

From the time you start writing a grant until you submit or the due date, you need to have everything at your fingertips.

It is now time to start collecting documents.

I always recommend that people write their first grant themselves. Why? For the very same reason. It takes a while to collect all the documents needed to be grant-ready.

As you write your first grant, large or small, you will start collecting. Even the boiler plate pieces about who will be managing grant funds at your organization and resumes take time to put together.

You simply have to stay organized. Create folders for your organization or for your grant writing clients. Every time your nonprofit, business, or you as an individual, is written about in print, put that in a folder. All published statistics belong in the folder.

If you're dealing with a healthcare organization, and you have access to the statistics for your target audience or community, put it in the folder.

Your folder should be saved externally, like on the Cloud, and/or a thumb drive. I also recommend that you maintain a hard copy of everything on your desk.

Even if your tax-exempt status is pending with the IRS, this Folders section will help you be ready when the letter arrives.

You will want to have your licenses to operate (if that is required), your building plans, the square footage of the rooms you will be using, etc. The list goes on and on, because the requirements of each funding source and every applicant is different. I have made checklists for you -- and where applicable to your organization or client – place each item in the folder.

So, let's prepare to be grant-ready with these 5 folders.

- Folder of Legal and Registrations

- Folder of Community Needs Data

- Folder of Organizational Support

- Folder of Organizational Capacity & Strengths

- Folder of Fiscal Management

Folders of Legal & Registrations

- ✓ Federal Tax Identification Number (EIN)

- ✓ Corporate documents

- ✓ IRS Federal Exemption Organization (EO) 501(c)(3) determination letter

- ✓ Copies of the org's IRS 990 filings

- ✓ Tax and financial data. (Most recent annual and quarterly financial/audit statements)

- ✓ SAM (Single Award Management) registration - Have you registered with SAM? As of April 4, to apply for federal grants, you need to be registered with SAM.gov. In addition, you need your Unique Entity ID is a 12-character alphanumeric ID assigned to an entity by SAM.gov

- ✓ Unique Entity ID

- ✓ ITP Cage number – To receive a Cage Code, your business must complete a registration within SAM.gov (System for Award Management)

- ✓ Operating licenses

- ✓ Lease or building title and equipment ownership.

- ✓ Building blueprints or floor plans

- ✓ Government related rules and regs of agencies

- ✓ Business/organizational Charter or State Article of Incorporation

- ✓ State Charitable Registration Number

- ✓ State Vendor Number- doing business in (state name)

Folder of Community Needs Data

- ✓ Community and neighborhood statistics

- ✓ Best practices and quotes from primary sources

- ✓ Target audience stats

- ✓ Newspaper articles showing needs

- ✓ Literature to quote

- ✓ Studies conducted

- ✓ Internal surveys

- ✓ Anything that documents the need, from news sources and any newspapers to online news outlet sources covering your organization

Folder of Organizational Support

- ✓ Table of Organization

- ✓ Programmatic Table of Organization

- ✓ In-kind Support Budget

- ✓ Programmatic Budget

- ✓ Description of management structure

- ✓ Gantt Chart - Timeline

- ✓ Organization Annual Calendar

- ✓ Key staff members FTEs paid and volunteers

- ✓ CVs, staff resumes of current key staff

- ✓ Current Job Descriptions

- ✓ TBA – Job Descriptions

- ✓ Letters of Support

- ✓ Memorandums of Understanding

- ✓ Skilled resources to devote to grant development (either in-house, contracted, or a combination of these)

Folder of Organizational Capacity & Strengths

- ✓ List of awards and recognitions

- ✓ List of current and previously funded grants (if applicable)

- ✓ Programmatic descriptions for programs and services offered or proposed.

- ✓ Good press – positive articles written about your organization's programs or key staff members.

- ✓ Text of previously written grant applications – both funded and not funded.

- ✓ Organization's promotional materials.

- ✓ Fundraising letters

- ✓ Your website and image of home page

- ✓ Organizational Capacity (one paragraph)

- ✓ Organizational History, one paragraph and expanded

- ✓ Organizational Bylaws - with updates and other governing documents

- ✓ Organization mission & vision statements

- ✓ Organization goals and objectives

- ✓ Organization population served

- ✓ Organizational measured outcomes for impact on your community

✓

Folder of Fiscal Management

✓ Boilerplate piece explaining fiscal management of organization

✓ Organization protocols statement and grants management process

✓ Annual current year budget

✓ Audited Financial Report

✓ Financial statements for budgets below $300,000 annually

✓ Financial statements for prior 2-3 years

✓ Projected budget and business plan for the organization

✓ Annual income and expenses, Profit and loss statements and Bank statements

You Won!!! Celebrate

If you were successful in winning a grant, take a moment to celebrate! It is a great feeling knowing all your hard work has now paid off!

Thank the funding source for giving your organization the opportunity and resources. Plan to reach out every 3 to 6 months with something positive.

Remember to congratulate your team and everyone who pitched in to help write your winning grant proposal.

And finally, with the funding source's permission, share your news in a press release and on social media platforms.

So, what happens next? The funding source's letter will indicate the funding distribution schedule. Since each funding source operates differently, the time from your notification about your win to receiving the actual grant funds will vary. Do not spend any money or oblige your organization before the funds arrive.

Grant award - confirm all the details.

Before accepting the grant money, you want to confirm the details of the agreement and what you are required to complete and accomplish. Get your team in order. Assign clear roles for each team member, such as who will be responsible for audits, reports, updates, etc.

Open a separate bank account.

Usually, when you win a grant, opening a separate account is a common prerequisite. However, if it is not, I still strongly advise it. Before the arrival date of the funds, you want to open a separate organization checking account, nicknamed according to the title of the grant or funding source.

Having a second bank account helps to keep the grant money separate from any other funding you might have. Further, it prevents accounting errors that result from the comingling of funds. Most importantly, maintain accurate records.

A grant is a gift with strings. If you created a budget in your application, which most grants request, then you identified how every penny of your request will be spent.

The grant funds are earmarked according to that budget; these are allowable expenses. Only write checks from that account, and only for what has been listed in the approved budget.

If you are not following the budget, the money you spend can, and will, be charged back to the organization by the funder.

You may also find yourself facing legal and criminal issues since the unauthorized use of grant funds coming from a nonprofit organization, governed by the IRS, is against the law.

Your grant award will not be private.

When you get funded, there will be several press releases sent to multiple media outlets. Many people within the community will take notice and they will be observing how you manage the program funds.

Next steps

Set up any pre-evaluation tests and administer them before starting the program. Another good idea is to create an advertisement for the TBD key program staff.

Write a press release announcement – obtain approval from the funding source before publication.

Budget modifications

You may only modify the grant budget with permission from the funding source.

For example, you budgeted a purchase of 20 laptops for your professional development program. The local computer store read about your program in the local newspaper and has offered an in-kind donation of 5 laptops for your program.

You may now be able to serve 5 additional people and that may cause you to need additional funds to further accommodate these five people. Or you may choose to use the funds no longer needed for the 5 laptops, continue serving the same number of people, and further enhance the program. You could re-appropriate the funds for something else, like a smartboard, for in-class teaching.

Before you move forward, you must contact the funding source and ask for permission to make the budget modification.

In most cases, when the new expense enhances the program without increasing the budget, and the item is not for anything the funding source stated in the grant application that they will not fund, permission will be granted.

When a grant is awarded, it's a gift given under the conditions that you spend the funds according to how you presented the budget.

There are strict guidelines on what you can and cannot spend your awarded money on after winning a grant. Consequently, if you spend funds on something without the approval of the funding source, you may have to return all of the grant award.

Never appropriate any funds other than those approved in the budget, without written permission from the funding source.

Submit all questions regarding allowable expenses to the funding source first. This is better than receiving a penalty for misrepresentation.

Many funders may ask for a midpoint and final report.

You don't want to end up with negative press for misappropriation of funds. We have all read those stories where money must be paid back, and someone gets arrested.

Audits, reports, and progress

To help manage the grant funding, grantors provide you with a list of what they need from you moving forward.

This list will include allowable/unallowable expenses and your reporting timelines. Furthermore, they may expect you to provide financial and programmatic reports. You may also have to give updates in presentations at organizational board meetings to show that things are on track, and you are spending the money responsibly in the way that was intended.

If some of the above is not requested of you, it is still a good opportunity to get into the practice for larger grants.

Keep a hard copy and an electronic copy.

Record all reports, receipts, obligations, and expenditures and store them in both hard copy and digital formats. The funding source can ask for proof of your expenses and request receipts at any time.

Any misrepresentation through delinquent or insufficient reporting may result in site visits, audits and possibly jail time, if determined to be fraudulent.

Meet the deadlines the funding source sets.

Keep on track with milestone deliverables for the duration of the grant. The key deliverable dates (reports, meetings, payments, etc.) must be strictly adhered to, so make sure they are NEVER overdue. Usually, there is a process you must follow if a project falls behind the agreed upon timeline.

Failure to abide by the stipulations set forth by the funding source can result in severe consequences, including the possibility of being banned from future award consideration by the funding source.

Build a positive relationship.

Aim to be accommodating, flexible, and consistent in your dealings with the funding source. This will set you on the right path from the get-go. For example, you could experience unexpected circumstances which may lead to a need for more grant modifications or extensions. Having a positive relationship with the funding source may provide you with more flexibility to deal with unforeseen issues.

Achieve, achieve, achieve.

Hit every milestone effortlessly and show that you and your team are capable and know your craft. If you can demonstrate high-quality execution in a timely manner, then additional grants will follow!

Review your results.

At the end of the term of a contract, you may need to return any unused grant money to the funding source. You should always review the data and determine the results of your program or project. Use that information to analyze areas of strength and weakness and determine where more or less funding is required.

Securing a grant is only half of the work. How will you sustain it when the funding ends? What will you do to disseminate your program? And is your program replicable in another area?

Sustainability

How will you sustain the program when the money runs out? The funding source wants to know how the program will continue into year two and three. Nobody likes a one year and done. How will you sustain the project after funding ends?

Describe the who, what, when where and how of your plan to find new funding opportunities. Include the structure of who is responsible at your organization for seeking additional funding sources.

State that your plan is to reduce dependence on a single funding source and to seek out diversified funding streams.

Write about how and where you will apply to additional funders. Describe your ongoing efforts to apply for additional grants and establish sustainable financial models. Mention any donor support pledged for next year, in-kind support from community and alumni support.

Collaborate with local organizations, local schools, community centers, higher educational institutions or government entities that share a similar mission to enhance program visibility, to share resources, expertise, and potentially secure additional funding through partnerships.

Include that you will be applying for funding from multiple sources, including local businesses, philanthropic organizations, and potential partnerships with other nonprofit organizations.

Write about local community engagement activities.

Talk about how your organization will continue to invest in professional development for best practices. How professional development will empower current staff to enhance their skills and become turn-key trainers for new staff, to continue the program long-term.

Include how your careful evaluation of your program will make it attractive to future funders. Show that the organization is prepared to adapt and evolve according to the evaluation.

You can also highlight cost-saving measures you will take to minimize operational costs while maintaining high-quality services. Include any sustainable practices within the program, such as energy-efficient equipment and eco-friendly initiatives.

Explain the steps to continue or close the program when the community needs change.

Dissemination – Sharing

How will you disseminate? How do you plan to publicize your grant award? How will you tell the world about your wonderful program? And how do you plan to disseminate your findings and evaluation?

The wider the reach of your proposed publicity, the more exciting and valuable your project will be to the funder.

In your grant application, you want to write the steps you will implement to disseminate and share your program. The goal is the replicability of your program to serve similar populations.

The secondary goal is to attract more donors and establish a niche within your industry for your organization.

Reach out to your volunteers, donors, partners, and the community you serve to become ambassadors of your program to share on social media.

Social media platforms allow for an incredible reach for spreading the word. All dissemination activities should be posted regularly. Newsletters, articles, and interviews will help you spread the word internally and externally.

Your organization can create joint activities with the funding source and your organization, like press releases, photo shoots, and podcast interviews.

Future volunteerism, donations, and partnerships depend on carefully cultivating and maintaining relationships. The impact of program activities and the outcomes and successes should be written about in trade magazines and validated with 30-second testimonial videos, which can be shared via social media.

Local newspapers and local television stations do an excellent job of writing about local programs that national media outlets can pick up.

Publicity brings new interest to both your organization and the funding source. All the excitement you generate can lead to similar organizations wanting to replicate your program to serve additional audiences in other locations.

Have you won a grant that you found on GrantWatch?

In recognition, I have a gift for you, for winning a grant that you found on GrantWatch. We only know that you have won a grant when you let us know.

GrantWatch will honor you with a gift of a free 17-ounce Latte Mug in recognition of your passion and diligent work.

At times, the GrantWatch PR team is able to secure a TV opportunity to highlight organizations that were awarded grants found on GrantWatch.

The staff also sets up in-person meetings with me when I am in your area. And at other times we do Zooms for podcasts with organizations that have won grants.

As a grant recipient, you will want to disseminate your program and share your success story. We post your testimonial videos on GrantWatch. Please take a moment to view these videos at the Media tab on GrantWatch. Watch how others have won actual grants.

Here are the simple details needed to receive a gift from GrantWatch:

- ✓ You must be able to verify your grant award for a grant that you found on GrantWatch.

- ✓ You must be able to meet with news organizations or podcasters via Skype, Zoom and/or Google.

- ✓ You must be able to be flexible to accommodate the news organization or a podcast producer's schedule.

- ✓ You must be willing to have your face, name, and company name on TV.

If you qualify, please send the information to support@GrantWatch.com. There is no guarantee of airtime, but you will definitely be considered. And you will receive a Latte Mug.

We hope media attention will bring additional funding for your organization.

Replicability

Is your program replicable? When writing the grant, you should keep this in mind. Can somebody in another state or another city model what you've developed and have successful outcomes?

We disseminate so that we can share the successes.

The goal is to create a model program that works and can be used repeatedly to serve your community and others, allowing for easy expansion to accommodate additional numbers of people and similar communities.

Identify key components that can be scaled up or down without compromising the program's effectiveness.

The findings from the outcomes and evaluation will direct the replication of your program.

Explain why you believe your program will be replicable in other locations for similar populations with similar needs. Be clear about what an organization will need to replicate the program.

You can implement a feedback loop that encourages continuous improvement based on insights from organizations replicating the program.

Explain who will be responsible for regularly updating the replication toolkit based on feedback and lessons learned.

Describe the strategic partnerships you plan to explore with educational institutions, nonprofits, or government agencies that may be interested in supporting the replication of the program.

And finally, collaborate with organizations that have expertise in scaling and replicating successful initiatives.

LIBBY HIKIND

IV: Modeling Successful Grants

Now that you have learned about mapping (in the previous section), it is time to look at the first blank page of your grant application with renewed confidence. The development of your program should now be less daunting when utilizing the mapping technique.

I want to show you how to create your map, so everything in your grant application flows and is easily understood by the reader.

Modeling the mapping process.

I am providing this sample map so you can "coast" through the first draft of your grant application. Feel free to use my sample map when writing your own grant. This model is for a large and lengthy grant application. Using the same procedure and pulling from the text the parts and pieces you want to include will help you develop any proposal.

Let's begin by calling our fictitious town Coastville. It's located in the mythical Grant County, California. Our imaginary nonprofit will be called Pre-Escolar Fantasia, and the fabricated funding source will be the Gelt4Good Foundation.

Pre-Escolar Fantasia wants to expand their existing preschool site and set up four new sites for EarlySchool preschool programming for a total of 5 sites for 500 children all across Coastville for the migrant children of Central America coming from Mexico, El Salvador, Guatemala, and Honduras.

Notice our map starts with Needs. This leads us to Goals, then we develop our Objectives and Activities. We conclude with the Evaluation.

As I create my map, I keep an excel document open or a plain notepad on the side to list all the items I will need to include in my budget. The map will keep all your answers in the grant application focused and aligned. Each of the charts are encompass a goal of your program.

Actual budget figures vary with each organization because they depend on local factors like rent per square foot, the negotiated teacher salaries, the cost of equipment, etc.

It's always beneficial to work with the financial experts at the organization and to consider local regulations. For example, in a preschool program there are specific requirements for space and bathroom facilities and in some jurisdictions the distance a school can be located from a gas station or dry cleaners is regulated. Keep all these requirements in mind when developing the budget.

To Facilitate Effective Communication: For the budget you will need to include either the costs or the value of in-kind support for interpreters and cultural liaisons for caregiver forums, meeting spaces or community centers for monthly forums, and the informational materials for caregivers.

NEEDS	GOALS	OBJECTIVES	ACTIVITIES	EVALUATION
Foreign-born residents in Coastville have diverse linguistic backgrounds, requiring effective communication strategies among caregivers to support the unique developmental needs of migrant children.	Facilitate Effective Communication	By the end of the school year, increase the percentage of caregivers who actively participate in communication workshops by 20%, aiming to enhance their ability to understand and support the unique developmental needs of migrant children.	Host monthly caregiver forums with interpreters and cultural liaisons to discuss the importance of effective communication in child development. Provide information about the upcoming preschool programs, address concerns, and gather feedback to refine communication strategies.	Monitor workshop attendance and survey caregivers to assess the effectiveness of the communication workshops. Measure the increase in caregivers' understanding of developmental needs through pre- and post-workshop assessments.

To Create a Secure and Supportive Environment: For the budget you will need to include either the costs or the value of in-kind support for teachers' and support staff salaries and benefits for the preschool program, appropriate classroom spaces and outdoor play areas, and age-appropriate educational materials and supplies.

NEEDS	GOALS	OBJECTIVES	ACTIVITIES	EVALUATION
Due to the high percentage of young residents in Coastville (nearly 27%), there is a need for a secure and supportive environment that caters to the specific developmental needs of children under 18.	**Create a Secure and Supportive Environment**	Implement age-appropriate, culturally sensitive activities in 100% of classrooms within the first quarter, fostering a sense of security and support for children under 18 in Coastville.	Organize a community event to showcase age-appropriate and culturally sensitive activities that will be integrated into the preschool programs. Invite families to participate, engage with educators, and experience firsthand the environment that will support their children's development.	Conduct regular classroom observations and gather feedback from both teachers and parents to assess the implementation of age-appropriate and culturally sensitive activities. Measure the perceived sense of security and support among children through surveys.

To Prioritize Language Development: For the budget you will need to include either the costs or the value of in-kind support for bilingual/multilingual educators and language development specialists, bilingual storybooks, educational games, and language resources, and for community outreach programs promoting language development.

NEEDS	GOALS	OBJECTIVES	ACTIVITIES	EVALUATION
Almost a quarter of households in Coastville are linguistically isolated, emphasizing the need to prioritize language development and provide bilingual/multilingual support for effective communication with families.	Prioritize Language Development	Increase the number of bilingual/multilingual resources and support services by 30% within the next six months, aiming to improve language development in linguistically isolated households in Coastville.	Conduct bilingual story time sessions in community spaces to promote language development and introduce families to the concept of bilingual/multilingual resources. Distribute materials highlighting the importance of language development and how it will be incorporated into the preschool programs.	Track the number of bilingual/multilingual resources added and assess their utilization. Conduct surveys or interviews with linguistically isolated households to gauge improvements in language development and communication.

To Cultivate an Inclusive Atmosphere: For the budget you will need to include either the costs or the value of in-kind support for event coordinators and support staff for the multicultural fair, venues for the fair, including stages and exhibition spaces, and promotional materials, cultural displays, and performances.

NEEDS	GOALS	OBJECTIVES	ACTIVITIES	EVALUATION
With over 50% of families living in poverty headed by married couples with children in Coastville, there is a need to cultivate an inclusive atmosphere that respects and supports the cultural and economic diversity within the community.	**Cultivate an Inclusive Atmosphere**	Develop and implement a cultural diversity program, engaging 80% of families living in poverty in Coastville within the next school year to promote inclusivity and understanding of diverse backgrounds.	Plan a multicultural fair in collaboration with local community groups. Encourage families to showcase their cultural heritage through food, performances, and displays. This activity will foster inclusivity and celebrate the diversity within Coastville, promoting a sense of community.	Monitor participation rates in the cultural diversity program and gather feedback from families involved. Conduct periodic assessments to measure the perceived inclusivity within the community and the understanding of diverse backgrounds.

To Provide Tailored Programs for Migrant Children: For the budget you will need to include either the costs or the value of in-kind support for qualified educators and specialists for tailored programs, ensure adequate classroom spaces with facilities for specific programs, specialized educational materials, toys, and learning aids.

NEEDS	GOALS	OBJECTIVES	ACTIVITIES	EVALUATION
As the study shows, children residing in Coastville face significant school readiness challenges, emphasizing the need for tailored preschool programs that address these challenges and align with city-wide school readiness goals.	**Tailored Programs for Migrant Children**	Achieve a 15% improvement in school readiness assessment scores for children in Coastville by the end of the school year, demonstrating the effectiveness of tailored preschool programs in addressing specific challenges.	Host a series of interactive workshops for parents and caregivers, providing insights into the tailored preschool programs. Share information on curriculum design, support services, and expected outcomes. Encourage active participation and address any concerns raised by families.	Analyze school readiness assessment scores before and after the implementation of tailored programs. Conduct teacher assessments and gather feedback from parents to evaluate the impact on children's readiness for kindergarten.

To Ensure Preparedness for Success: For the budget you will need to include either the costs or the value of in-kind support for transition coordinators and support staff for workshops, transition kits, informational packets, and resources and outreach efforts to engage Central American migrant families.

NEEDS	GOALS	OBJECTIVES	ACTIVITIES	EVALUATION
Nearly 40% of the Grant County's Central America's population lives in Coastville, indicating a need to ensure that preschool programs prepare Central American migrant children and their families for a successful transition to kindergarten.	**Ensure Preparedness for Success**	Increase the participation rate of Central American families in transition preparation workshops by 25% over the next two quarters, ensuring that every Central American child and family leaving the preschool program is well-prepared for success in kindergarten.	Organize transition preparation workshops specifically for Central American families. Provide resources, guidance, and information about the upcoming preschool programs. Facilitate meetings with kindergarten teachers to discuss expectations and create a seamless transition plan for the Central American children.	Track the participation rates in transition preparation workshops and assess the feedback from Central American families. Measure the perceived preparedness for kindergarten through pre- and post-workshop assessments and ongoing communication with kindergarten teachers.

Stats to Include in a Needs Section

Since the Needs Section must clearly show the existence of a problem. You will need to add relevant supporting data like demographics, economic health, education, crime, and safety.

Please remember that this entire chapter contains fictitious data and statements and was only written to provide a model for writing grants. Nothing in this chapter should ever be quoted as facts.

Sample Needs to Include

The data provided will convincingly demonstrate the need for the expansion of EarlySchool Programs in the Coastville.

The evidence is strong that high-quality Pre-Kindergarten can have significant short- and long-term impacts on children and their communities.

The long-term benefits of high-quality Pre-K programs are documented in well-known longitudinal studies. The Pre-K Study, a rigorous scientific study of Pre-K programs in Grant County, revealed students who attended high-quality early education programs experienced greater academic success and educational attainment (Child Development Book, 2021).

Coastville is a town that hosts many impoverished families. Fifty Percent (50% or more) of Coastville families are living in poverty headed by married couples with young children, many of which have two working adults.

According to 2023 data published by Grant County's Office of Academic Achievement and the Office of Planning, Coastville demonstrates a high need.

- Foreign-born residents in Coastville have diverse linguistic backgrounds, requiring effective communication strategies among caregivers to support the unique developmental needs of migrant children.

- Due to the high percentage of young residents in Coastville (nearly 27%), there is a need for a secure and supportive environment that caters to the specific developmental needs of children under 18.

- Almost a quarter of households in Coastville are linguistically isolated, emphasizing the need to prioritize language development and provide bilingual/multilingual support for effective communication with families.

- With over 50% of families living in poverty headed by married couples with children in Coastville, there is a need to cultivate an inclusive atmosphere that respects and supports the cultural and economic diversity within the community.

- As the study shows, children residing in Coastville face significant school readiness challenges, emphasizing the need for tailored preschool programs that address these challenges and align with city-wide school readiness goals.

- Nearly 40% of the Grant County's Central population lives in Coastville, indicating a need to ensure that preschool programs prepare Central American migrant children and their families for a successful transition to kindergarten.

Examples of Goals Section

Your program goals should always link to your needs statement. If you look at the maps presented on the previous pages you will have some excellent examples. It's worth noticing the language used in this section of your proposal.

The overall goal is to provide EarlySchool, a preschool program which caters to children from non-English speaking, two-parent migrant working families from Central America.

Pre-Escolar Fantasia wants to set up five sites for EarlySchool, for a total of 500 children all across Coastville for the migrant children of Central America coming from Mexico, El Salvador, Guatemala, and Honduras.

The organization will probably need to write multiple grants to supplement all the budgetary needs.

Goals

As a full day pre-school program, we will have the opportunity to extend our students' high-quality learning opportunities that meet the city-wide school readiness goals and the State P-12 Common Core Learning Standards.

To establish an overarching goal that ensures that every migrant child, when age appropriate, will leave our early childhood program and enter kindergarten ready to succeed, using best practices in developmentally appropriate early childhood education services. By incorporating the specific needs of Coastville children into each goal, the Pre-Escolar Fantasia EarlySchool preschool program aims to address the challenges faced by the diverse population in that community.

Our goals are:

- To facilitate effective communication among caregivers, recognizing and embracing the diverse cultural and linguistic backgrounds of migrant children, including those in Coastville, to better understand and support their unique developmental needs.

- To create a secure and supportive environment that is sensitive to the experiences of migrant children in Coastville, emphasizing culturally relevant and age-appropriate activities that foster a sense of belonging.

- To prioritize language development with a focus on bilingual and multilingual support, acknowledging the linguistic diversity within the migrant community, particularly in Coastville, and providing resources to enhance communication skills.

- To cultivate an inclusive atmosphere that respects and celebrates the rich cultural heritage of migrant children in Coastville, promoting socialization and a sense of community.

- To develop comprehensive, full-day preschool programs tailored to meet the specific educational and transitional needs of migrant children, including those facing school readiness challenges in Coastville. To align these programs with city-wide school readiness goals and the State P-12 Common Core Learning Standards.

- To establish an overarching goal to ensure that every migrant child and family transitioning from our early childhood programs, especially those in Coastville, enters kindergarten fully prepared for success. Integrate best practices in developmentally appropriate early childhood education services tailored to their unique circumstances.

Needs Assessment and Your Hook

When it comes to grant proposals, capturing the attention of reviewers is crucial for success. Crafting a compelling hook in your grant proposal will engage reviewers from the start. Just like a captivating opening scene in a film, a well-crafted hook can draw the reader in and make them eager to learn more. Let's explore some strategies for crafting a compelling hook that will pique the interest of reviewers and set your proposal apart.

Start with a Powerful Statement: Begin your hook with a thought-provoking statement or a surprising statistic relevant to your preschool programs. For example, if you are seeking support for a your EarlySchool program which will address language development, you could open with a statement like, "In Coastville, almost a quarter of households are linguistically isolated." This statement immediately captures attention and underscores the significance of your program.

Here is another possible hook: If you are writing about effective communication, you could open with a statement like, "In Coastville, where foreign-born residents make up more than 45% of the population, effective communication among caregivers is crucial."

Tell a Captivating Story

Humans are hardwired to respond to stories, so why not incorporate storytelling into your hook? Share a brief anecdote or case study that demonstrates the problem you are addressing that illustrates the unique needs addressed by your tailored preschool program.

For instance, in Coastville, a touching story could revolve around a migrant family navigating their language and how they rely on the few words their young children have learned in the local playground. You can connect emotionally with the Gelt4Good Foundation, by creating a compelling reason for them to continue exploring the significance of your preschool initiatives. This will propel them to continue reading.

Highlight a Gap or Need: Identify a gap or need by addressing the specific needs of migrant children in Coastville. This can be a powerful way to engage with the Gelt4Good Foundation. Emphasize the current gaps in accessible and culturally sensitive early childhood education for this demographic. When you highlight the gap, you explain the importance of your project and demonstrate its potential impact in filling a crucial need.

Remember that there will be other similar organizations vying for the same available funds. What makes your organization best positioned to fill that need?

Pose an Intriguing Question: Open your hook with a thought-provoking question that sparks curiosity in the reviewer's mind. Pose an intriguing question relating to the tailored preschool programs for migrant children in Coastville. For example, you could ask, "What if we could create an educational environment that not only addresses the unique needs of migrant children but also empowers them for a seamless transition to kindergarten?" This question immediately captures attention and sets the stage for the innovative and impactful approach of your preschool program you are proposing.

Share a Startling Fact: Present a surprising or little-known fact that underscores the significance of the tailored preschool programs for migrant children in Coastville. For example, you could begin with a startling fact like, "In Coastville, where over 50% of families living in poverty are actually headed by married couples with children, sadly access to quality early childhood education is limited, hindering the developmental opportunities for young minds." This fact creates a sense of urgency and emphasizes the critical need for immediate action in implementing our innovative preschool initiatives.

Remember, your hook should be concise, and relevant to the unique needs of Coastville. It should not only grab the attention of the reader but also align with the overall goals and objectives of Pre-Escolar Fantasia. By crafting a compelling hook, you increase the chances of engaging the grant reviewer and motivating them to explore the significance of your tailored preschool initiatives.

Example of a Hook

Unleashing the Potential of Coastville's Children. At Pre-Escolar Fantasia, our hearts beat with an unwavering passion for empowering children and families to thrive. We are bursting with enthusiasm as we present our groundbreaking program, a transformative journey that will ignite a brighter future for the communities we serve. Brace yourself for a heartfelt glimpse into our vision.

Imagine a world where every child can unlock their full potential, where educational and health disparities become relics of the past. Our proposed program aims to transcend boundaries, to uplift the lives of 500 children and families residing in the large Central American migrant community of Coastville, California. It's a rallying cry, a call to action to reshape the trajectory of their lives.

With an unyielding commitment, we envision Pre-Escolar Fantasia's EarlySchool Programs will span across six service areas within Coastville. We cannot in good conscience accept the status quo, for there is an urgent need to bridge the gaps in preschool access. It is our passion to cultivate a nurturing environment where every child can flourish, regardless of their background or circumstances.

As a result of our program, imagine children embarking on their educational journey with confidence and curiosity. As a result of our program, envision families embracing a newfound sense of hope, armed with the tools and resources to navigate life's challenges. We will measure our success not only in numbers but also in the radiant smiles, the spark of knowledge ignited, and the dreams rekindled.

Our activities will ripple through the community, leaving lasting imprints of progress. Through comprehensive assessments and data-driven approaches, we will chart the course towards success. Our dedicated team will employ a range of evaluation instruments, meticulously measuring the impact of our efforts. We will navigate uncharted territories, adapting our strategies as we glean insights from the lives we touch.

Our program is more than just a grant proposal; it is an embodiment of our unwavering passion, a testament to the limitless potential of each child we serve. We invite you to join us on this awe-inspiring journey, where hope becomes reality and dreams find wings to soar. There is a great opportunity here to use our combined compassion to empower the migrant children and families who live in Coastville.

Together, let's unlock a future where every child's brilliance shines through.

Example of Needs Section

Pre-Escolar Fantasia stands before you today, driven by an unwavering commitment to the children and families of Coastville, California. With the desire of an educator looking to transform lives, we present a groundbreaking proposal to meet the educational needs of 500 deserving children and their families. Through an ambitious expansion of our services in Coastville, including the enhancement of our current childcare site and the establishment of four additional sites, we aim to unlock the untapped potential within our community.

Within the heart of Coastville lies a call that cannot be ignored; a call for urgent action to increase access to the Pre-Escolar Fantasia's EarlySchool Program. A comprehensive assessment conducted by our dedicated team, consisting of center staff, parents, governing body members, and an independent contractor, has unveiled a startling reality. While the demand for Pre-Escolar Fantasia's EarlySchool Program services spans across 11 zip codes within Coastville, only three currently possess the capacity to provide this vital support. The time to bridge this gap is now.

Looking at the data for this vibrant and diverse community, we find ourselves confronted by staggering statistics that reveal the pressing need for intervention. An estimated 2000 children from families with little or no English proficiency reside within

Coastville, their potential stifled by limited opportunities for growth and development. Shockingly, there are many reported cases of child neglect each year, when parents go to work leaving their young children unattended due to lack of preschool slots. There is an urgent cry for change. Coastville has large areas of unserved and underserved residents who bear the weight of lack of language, unmet educational and childcare needs, yearning for a brighter tomorrow.

Here you would add a paragraph of the demographic statistics for the community.

Only 25% of the estimated three to five-year-olds in Coastville have had the privilege of enrolling in some form of preschool.

We cannot ignore the harsh realities that encircle the Coastville community, where the estimated median household income of $25,000 lingers below the poverty line. An overwhelming poverty rate of 50% for the service area in 2022 further accentuates the urgency of our mission.

Today, we stand at the crossroads of possibility, poised to unlock the potential of Coastville's children. By expanding our Pre-Escolar Fantasia's EarlySchool Program, we will transform their lives, fueling a ripple effect that will reverberate through generations. Together, let's empower these young minds and provide them with the education they deserve.

Example of Activities Section

These activities aim to engage the Coastville community, build awareness about the upcoming preschool programs, and address the specific objectives outlined for each goal. Through these initiatives, the goal of opening five preschool programs for 500 migrant children can be achieved while meeting the unique needs of Coastville's population.

Facilitate Effective Communication: Host monthly caregiver forums with interpreters and cultural liaisons to discuss the importance of effective communication in child development. Provide information about the upcoming preschool programs, address concerns, and gather feedback to refine communication strategies.

Create a Secure and Supportive Environment: Organize a community event to showcase age-appropriate and culturally sensitive activities that will be integrated into the preschool programs. Invite families to participate, engage with educators, and experience firsthand the environment that will support their children's development.

Prioritize Language Development: Conduct bilingual story time sessions in community spaces to promote language development and introduce families to the concept of bilingual/multilingual resources. Distribute materials that highlight the importance of language development and how it will be incorporated into preschool programs.

Cultivate an Inclusive Atmosphere: Plan a multicultural fair in collaboration with local community groups. Encourage families to showcase their cultural heritage through food, performances, and displays. This activity will foster inclusivity and celebrate the diversity within Coastville, promoting a sense of community.

Tailored Programs for Migrant Children: Host a series of interactive workshops for parents and caregivers, providing insights into the tailored preschool programs. Share information on curriculum design, support services, and expected outcomes. Encourage active participation and address any concerns raised by families.

Ensure Preparedness for Success: Organize transition preparation workshops specifically for South American families. Provide resources, guidance, and information about the upcoming preschool programs. Facilitate meetings with kindergarten teachers to discuss expectations and create a seamless transition plan for the South American children.

Example of Evaluation Section

Here's an overview of how each objective can be measured and the instruments that can be used for evaluation. Regular assessments, feedback mechanisms, and data collection will be crucial in evaluating the success of each objective. Adjustments to strategies and interventions can be made based on the evaluation results to ensure continuous improvement in meeting the needs of the Coastville community.

Here's an evaluation of each objective:

Facilitate Effective Communication: Monitor workshop attendance and survey caregivers to assess the effectiveness of the communication workshops. Measure the increase in caregivers' understanding of developmental needs through pre- and post-workshop assessments.

Create a Secure and Supportive Environment: Conduct regular classroom observations and gather feedback from both teachers and parents to assess the implementation of age-appropriate and culturally sensitive activities. Measure the perceived sense of security and support among children through surveys.

Prioritize Language Development: Track the number of bilingual/multilingual resources added and assess their utilization. Conduct surveys or interviews with linguistically isolated households to gauge improvements in language development and communication.

Cultivate an Inclusive Atmosphere: Monitor participation rates in the cultural diversity program and gather feedback from families involved. Conduct periodic assessments to measure the perceived inclusivity within the community and the understanding of diverse backgrounds.

Tailored Programs for Migrant Children: Analyze school readiness assessment scores before and after the implementation of tailored programs. Conduct teacher assessments and gather feedback from parents to evaluate the impact on children's readiness for kindergarten.

Ensure Preparedness for Success: Track the participation rates in transition preparation workshops and assess the feedback from South American families. Measure the perceived preparedness for kindergarten through pre- and post-workshop assessments and ongoing communication with kindergarten teachers.

Example of Organizational Capacity Section

Your organizational capacity section should instill trust and confidence in your organization's financial management capabilities. Your program should be a source of pride for the foundation, and they should feel honored to be associated with it.

Pre-Escolar Fantasia possesses a strong organizational capacity, and is well-positioned to deliver effective programs, expand its reach, and make a positive impact on the lives of children and families in Coastville.

Pre-Escolar Fantasia has a strong organizational capacity that enables it to effectively deliver its programs and services. Here are some key aspects of its organizational capacity:

Experienced Staff: Pre-Escolar Fantasia has a dedicated and experienced team of professionals who are knowledgeable in early childhood education, child development, and program management. The staff members possess the necessary qualifications, skills, and expertise to deliver high-quality services to children and families.

Established Infrastructure: The organization has well-equipped facilities, including its main office and multiple childcare sites, which are conducive to providing a safe and enriching environment for children. These sites have age-appropriate learning materials, play areas, and resources to support the Pre-Escolar Fantasia's EarlySchool Program.

Strong Governance and Leadership: Pre-Escolar Fantasia operates under the guidance of a competent governing body that provides strategic direction and oversight. The board of directors consists of individuals with diverse backgrounds and expertise who are committed to the organization's mission and the well-being of the children and families it serves.

Collaborative Partnerships: The organization has established partnerships with local stakeholders, community organizations, and service providers, creating a network of support that enhances its capacity to meet the educational needs of children and families. These partnerships allow for resource sharing, referrals, and coordinated efforts to maximize impact.

Robust Program Management: Pre-Escolar Fantasia employs effective program management strategies, including monitoring and evaluation systems, to ensure the efficient implementation of its programs. It regularly assesses program outcomes, collects data, and utilizes feedback to continuously improve its services and adapt to the evolving needs of the community.

Financial Sustainability: The organization demonstrates financial stability and sustainability through diversified funding sources, including grants, donations, and partnerships. It maintains sound fiscal management practices, budgeting, and reporting systems to ensure transparency and accountability.

Continuous Professional Development: Pre-Escolar Fantasia invests in the professional development of its staff through ongoing training, workshops, and conferences. This ensures that the organization remains up to date with the latest research, best practices, and innovations in early childhood education.

Examples of Timelines Section

Excel has a variety of Gantt Charts to choose from. Go to excel and choose new and type in Gantt.

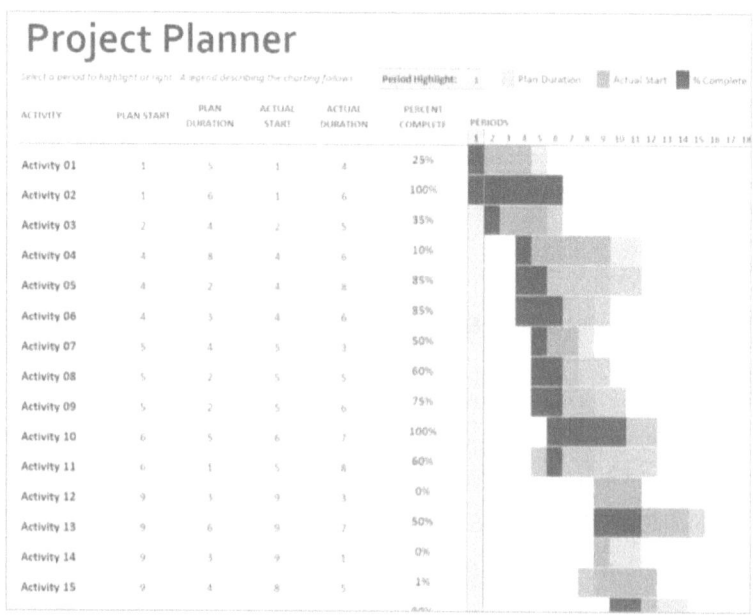

I would change the column headings, so you have room to add a column for the person(s) responsible. The beauty is you can cut and paste your activities and then insert rows for all the details.

Timeline

ACTIVITY	Person(s) Responsible	Weeks 1	2	3	4	5	6	7	8	9	10	11	12	13	14
Pre-Escolar Fantasia receives the grant award notification.		X													
Project team celebrates and acknowledges the funding.		X	X												
Project team conducts a kick-off meeting to discuss the program's goals, objectives, and deliverables.		X	X												
Detailed program planning takes place, including resource allocation, timeline development, and identification of key stakeholders.		X		X		X		X							
Program staff and partners collaborate to finalize the curriculum, parent education, and program implementation strategies.			X		X		X		X						

Here are some major activities and milestones you might want to add to your timeline, from the receipt of the grant award to the evaluation and report:

- ✓ Pre-Escolar Fantasia receives the grant award notification.
- ✓ Project team celebrates and acknowledges the funding.

- ✓ Project team conducts a kick-off meeting to discuss the program's goals, objectives, and deliverables.

- ✓ Detailed program planning takes place, including resource allocation, timeline development, and identification of key stakeholders.

- ✓ Program staff and partners collaborate to finalize the curriculum and program implementation strategies.

- ✓ Project team establishes evaluation framework and indicators for measuring progress and outcomes.

- ✓ Pre-Escolar Fantasia initiates the recruitment process for additional staff, ensuring they meet the required qualifications.

- ✓ Staff undergo comprehensive training on the Pre-Escolar Fantasia's EarlySchool Program curriculum, health and safety protocols, and program guidelines.

- ✓ Training sessions may include workshops, seminars, and on-the-job training to build the capacity of the program staff.

- ✓ Pre-Escolar Fantasia launches the Pre-Escolar Fantasia's EarlySchool Program at each designated site in Coastville.

- ✓ Daily activities and lessons are delivered to children, focusing on early education, social-emotional development, and health promotion.

- ✓ Ongoing monitoring of program activities takes place, including regular staff meetings, observations, and assessments of children's progress.

- ✓ Partnerships and collaborations with community organizations are strengthened to enhance program effectiveness and reach.

- ✓ Pre-Escolar Fantasia collects data on program implementation, child outcomes, and family engagement.

- ✓ Evaluation instruments, such as surveys, assessments, and observation tools, are utilized to gather quantitative and qualitative data.

- ✓ Data analysis is conducted to measure progress against the program's objectives and evaluate the program's impact.

- ✓ The evaluation process includes regular check-ins, data review, and feedback sessions with staff, parents, and key stakeholders.

- ✓ Pre-Escolar Fantasia compiles the evaluation findings and prepares a comprehensive program report.

- ✓ The report highlights the program's achievements, challenges, lessons learned, and recommendations for future improvements.

- ✓ The report is submitted to the grant provider, stakeholders, and other relevant parties as required.

- ✓ Project team members participate in dissemination activities, such as presenting findings at conferences or sharing the report with the wider community.

It's important to note that the timeline provided is a general framework, and the specific duration of each phase will vary depending on the program's scope, resources, and any unforeseen circumstances. Regular communication, collaboration, and flexibility among the project team and stakeholders are crucial to ensure successful implementation and evaluation of the Pre-Escolar Fantasia's EarlySchool Program in Coastville.

Example of Budget Section

The budget narrative clearly itemizes how you arrived at the budget and exactly what budgeted items will be covered by the grant, and what items will be covered by matching funds or in-kind donations.

When I write a budget narrative, I take the entire row in excel and explain how I got to the number. I write each sentence like this: "Funds have been requested for rent of 5 buildings, for 10 classrooms per building of 960 square feet per classroom, @$14.65 per square foot for a total of $703,200."

However, when I finish calculating my budget, I may determine that my needs for 50 classrooms to serve 500 children is way more than the grant will fund with all the other items like teacher salaries, materials, evaluation consultant, etc.

Now I have to revisit my Excel budget spreadsheet which should be chock full of equations that let me re-calculate quickly and say, "What if we have 20 students in each classroom? I will need less rental space and equipment. Now I need to add assistant teachers and possibly a part time aide per classroom."

Unfortunately, now I may need to revise my detailed pictorial organization table. I may need to revise my LOI or my full application.

Maybe I should revisit the 500 number and serve less students. Five hundred may be an overreach. Five sites may be too much.

So, what did I do wrong, here? If I am now working on my budget, close to deadline, after writing my entire grant I am doomed! If you first draft your budget, your entire grant application will flow.

What comes to mind is the last set of grants that I wrote, before I retired from grant writing. I had five clients that knew each other well and I received permission to write a grant for all of them. The grant was being offered to many organizations, so they were not in tight competition.

I seem to remember that they all got together the night before the deadline at some event or had a group call or some meeting and I received 5 calls the next morning. All of them were changing their budgets and adding items and additional personnel. The excel spreadsheet was not the problem. The grant application was.

I have brought you to this point in the modeling section of the book to show you what can and will happen. Every place I wrote "500 children" will have to change. Every place where I wrote "5 sites" or drew "10 classrooms", and the total budget numbers in the LOI and countless more places will need to be changed. And what if you wanted to increase instead of decreasing?

What my clients wanted was impossible. I was working on a federal grant and each application was already 100 pages long. Every item in the budget was mentioned in the document. A reader would not think for a minute when looking at the budget about why this or that is needed.

I warned them, but the customer is always right. However, in this case, I put my warnings in writing. None of these grants were funded. I got paid, but I felt bad because I like to win, and they lost out. We did use their grant applications to apply for other funding. Still, they lost time, and my fee. All five clients learned an unbelievably valuable lesson.

I remember my old School District office and the adding machine. Before a grant was considered, we back tracked into a number to know how many we can serve, and what services we could provide within the amount we believed we could safely request from that funder.

Today, grant writers are lucky to have excel and the ability to create formulas within a spreadsheet, so you change the number of classrooms or students or teachers and the entire budget will instantaneously recalculate.

If you do not know how to use excel, invest the time, and do something more familiar to you. Calculate your own personal family budget, write formulas and you will start to get the hang of it. Again, you do not want to be learning, at deadline.

Here is an opening for your budget narrative. Below each or within each paragraph explain each row in your Excel budget as I showed you above with rental space.

Pre-Escolar Fantasia is committed to ensuring the effective implementation of the Pre-Escolar Fantasia's EarlySchool Program in Coastville. The budget outlined below provides a comprehensive overview of the anticipated expenses and in-kind support required to successfully conduct the program.

Personnel Expenses:

Salaries: The budget includes funds for program staff, including teachers, administrative personnel, and support staff. These individuals will be responsible for program coordination, curriculum delivery, administration, and monitoring. The salaries are based on industry standards and will be in line with local regulations and organizational policies.

Benefits: In addition to salaries, the budget allocates funds for employee benefits, such as healthcare, retirement contributions, and paid leave. These benefits are essential for attracting and retaining qualified staff members.

Program Materials and Supplies:

Curriculum Resources: Funds are allocated to purchase age-appropriate educational materials, books, manipulatives, and learning aids for the program. These resources will enhance the quality of instruction and provide engaging and interactive learning experiences for the children.

Health and Safety Supplies: The budget includes provisions for the purchase of necessary supplies, including first aid kits, cleaning supplies, hygiene products, and safety equipment. These supplies will ensure the health and well-being of the children and maintain a safe program environment.

Facility Enhancements:

Renovation and Maintenance: The budget includes funds for necessary renovations and maintenance of the program sites in Coastville. This may include repairs, upgrades, and improvements to ensure the facilities meet health and safety standards and provide a conducive learning environment.

Professional Development and Training:

Workshops and Seminars: Funds are allocated for staff professional development activities, including workshops, seminars, and conferences. These opportunities will enhance the skills and knowledge of program staff, ensuring high quality instruction and effective implementation of the Pre-Escolar Fantasia's EarlySchool Program.

Evaluation and Reporting:

Data Collection and Analysis: The budget includes resources for data collection tools, software, and analysis to measure program outcomes and evaluate its impact. These expenses will support the comprehensive evaluation process and enable accurate reporting on the program's effectiveness.

Reporting and Dissemination: Funds are allocated for the preparation and dissemination of program reports, including printing, graphic design, and distribution costs. These activities will ensure the program's accomplishments are effectively communicated to stakeholders, policymakers, and the broader community.

In-Kind Support:

Pre-Escolar Fantasia is grateful for the valuable in-kind support received from various partners and stakeholders. This support contributes to the success of the Pre-Escolar Fantasia's EarlySchool Program and helps maximize the impact of the allocated budget. The in-kind support includes:

- Donated educational materials, books, and learning resources from community organizations and individuals.

- Volunteer hours from parents, community members, and professionals who contribute their time and expertise to support program activities.

- Shared facilities or reduced rent agreements with partner organizations, minimizing facility expenses.

- Pro bono services from consultants, experts, or professionals who provide their expertise and guidance without charge.

Pre-Escolar Fantasia will maintain a detailed record of the in-kind support received, including the estimated value of each contribution, to accurately reflect the overall resources invested in the program.

Overall, the budget and in-kind support outlined above demonstrate Pre-Escolar Fantasia's commitment to responsibly manage the funds and resources to achieve the desired outcomes of the Pre-Escolar Fantasia's EarlySchool Program in Coastville.

Example of Fiscal Management Section

Fiscal Management:

Pre-Escolar Fantasia is dedicated to ensuring strong fiscal management and accountability in the implementation of the Pre-Escolar Fantasia's EarlySchool Program in Coastville. The organization recognizes the importance of efficient financial practices to maximize the impact of grant funds and maintain transparency. The fiscal management plan is outlined below:

Budget Development and Monitoring:

Pre-Escolar Fantasia will establish a budget development process that involves input from key stakeholders, including program staff, administrators, and finance personnel. The budget will be comprehensive, aligning with the program goals and objectives, and adhere to any specific guidelines or requirements set by the grant provider.

A designated finance team will be responsible for monitoring the budget throughout the program's implementation. Regular budget reviews and tracking of expenses will ensure adherence to the approved budget and enable timely adjustments as needed.

Financial Policies and Procedures:

Pre-Escolar Fantasia will maintain clear and well-defined financial policies and procedures. These policies will cover areas such as procurement, expense reimbursement, financial reporting, and internal controls. They will be communicated to all relevant staff members and regularly reviewed and updated, as necessary.

Adequate financial controls will be implemented to safeguard the grant funds and ensure compliance with applicable laws, regulations, and grant requirements. This includes measures such as segregation of duties, proper documentation of financial transactions, and regular internal audits.

Grant Fund Disbursement:

Pre-Escolar Fantasia will establish a system for efficient and accountable disbursement of grant funds. This will include the development of a grant payment schedule, ensuring that funds are released in a timely manner and in accordance with the approved budget.

The organization will maintain proper documentation for all financial transactions related to the program, including invoices, receipts, and payment records. This documentation will be readily available for auditing and reporting purposes.

Financial Reporting:

Pre-Escolar Fantasia will prepare regular financial reports to track the utilization of grant funds. These reports will provide a detailed breakdown of expenses, comparing actual expenditures against the approved budget. The reports will be shared with the grant provider and other relevant stakeholders as required.

In addition to financial reports, Pre-Escolar Fantasia will provide narrative reports that highlight program achievements, challenges, and progress towards meeting program objectives. These reports will complement the financial information and provide a comprehensive overview of program performance.

The signing authority for checks at Pre-Escolar Fantasia will depend on the organization's internal financial policies and procedures. Typically, the authority to sign checks is designated to specific individuals within the organization who have the appropriate level of fiscal responsibility and oversight.

Commonly, the executive director or CEO of Pre-Escolar Fantasia will have signing authority for checks, along with the chief financial officer or finance manager. These individuals are responsible for ensuring that all financial transactions, including check disbursements, are conducted in accordance with the organization's policies and procedures.

It's important to note that the specific signing authority may vary based on the organization's internal structure and policies. Pre-Escolar Fantasia will establish clear guidelines regarding check signing authority to maintain proper financial controls and accountability.

Audit and Compliance:

Pre-Escolar Fantasia is committed to maintaining the highest standards of financial accountability and compliance. The organization will cooperate fully with any external audits or financial reviews conducted by the grant provider or other authorized entities.

Internal audits will be conducted regularly to assess financial practices, identify areas for improvement, and ensure compliance with organizational policies and grant requirements. Any findings or recommendations from these audits will be promptly addressed and corrective actions implemented.

Pre-Escolar Fantasia understands that effective fiscal management is crucial for the success of the Pre-Escolar Fantasia's EarlySchool Program. By implementing sound financial practices, maintaining transparency, and ensuring compliance, the organization aims to maximize the impact of grant funds and demonstrate responsible stewardship of resources.

Examples of Tables of Organization

A typical table of organizational structure is a pictorial view of the structure of responsibilities, supervision, and relationships within an organization.

When it is personal to you, it takes many drafts to get it right. Do not leave this to the end. Look for the existing table of organizational structure if there is one and start modifying it along the way. Just as you keep the budget open, keep the table open as you continue to list all the people you plan to hire in the new program.

You may decide to have two tables. One for your established organization with all the roles and departments and one depicting the structure of your proposed program in your grant application.

I like to draw it out using pencil and paper (with a large eraser) and hand it off to a graphic artist. You may have someone on staff who is very capable of designing a colorful table in PowerPoint.

It's important to consult the specific organizational documents, such as the bylaws or official documentation, for an accurate and up-to-date understanding of your organizational structure.

This list below are common roles and departments found in many organizations:

- Executive Leadership

- Chief Executive Officer (CEO)/Executive Director

- Chief Financial Officer (CFO)/Finance Director

- Chief Operating Officer (COO)/Operations Director

- Administrative and Support Departments

- Human Resources

- Finance and Accounting

- Information Technology

- Facilities and Office Management

- Program and Service Departments

- Early Childhood Education

- Health and Wellness

- Family Support Services

- Community Outreach and Engagement

- Operations and Logistics

- Program Managers/Coordinators

- Quality Assurance and Compliance

- Data Management and Evaluation

- Fundraising and Development

- Development Director

- Grant Writing and Donor Relations

- Events and Community Engagement

Table of Organization Samples

These samples are modified from previous grants I have written. They demonstrate both creativity and capacity. Be as creative and colorful as possible. Give your reader a visual picture of your organization and a break from reading paragraph after paragraph of text.

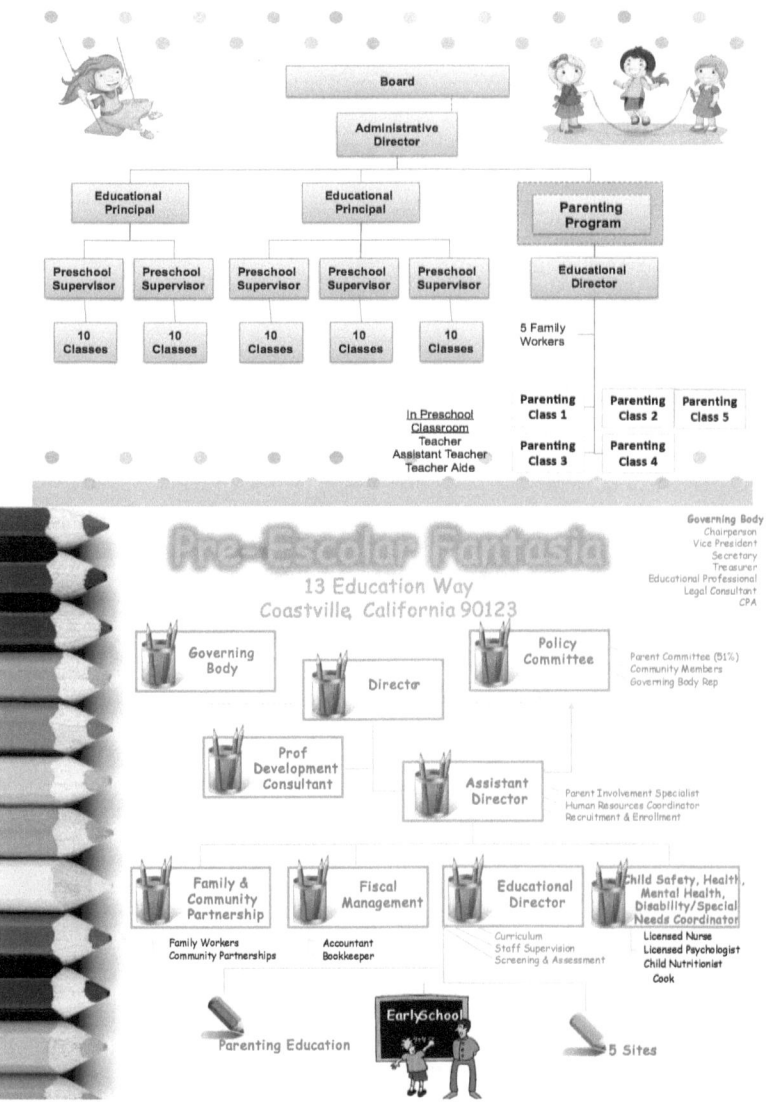

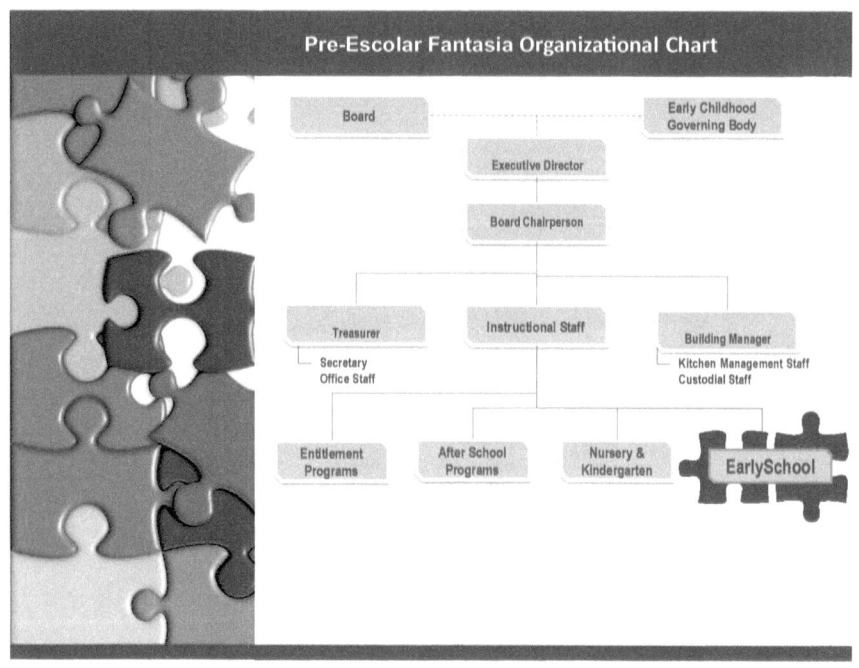
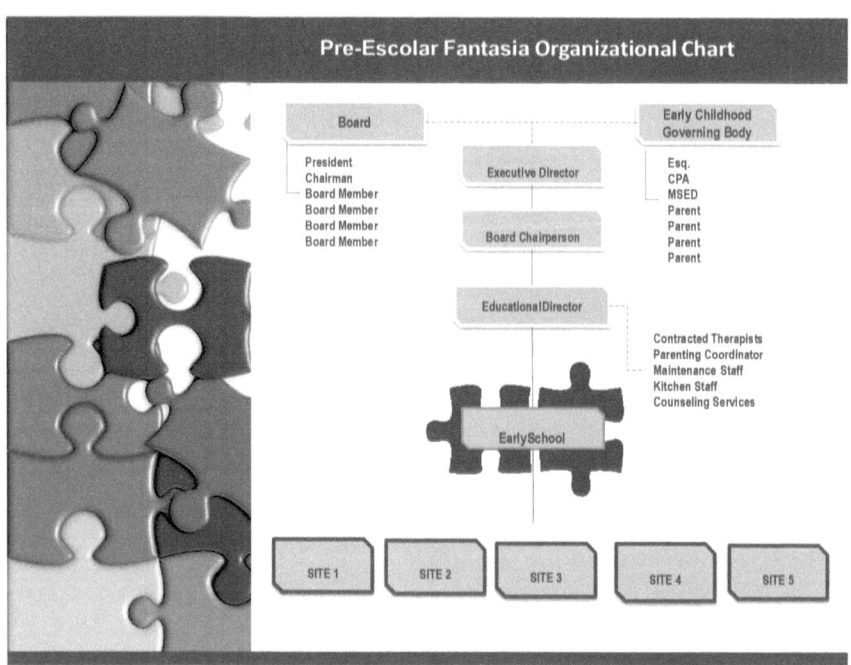

Example of a Letter of Inquiry

Pre-Escolar Fantasia

13 Education Way

Coastville, California 90123

January 24, 2024

Gelt4Good Foundation

18 MyCassa Drive

Bienvenido, California 90456

Subject: Letter of Inquiry for Expanding Pre-Escolar Fantasia's EarlySchool Preschool Program Across Coastville

Dear Director at Gelt4Good Foundation,

I am writing to express our organization's keen interest in Gelt4Good Foundation's initiatives to support education programs for migrant children. This Letter of Inquiry is a response to your Request for Proposals (RFP) for initiatives to educate the new migrant population.

Our organization, Pre-Escolar Fantasia, seeks support to expand our existing site and establish four new sites for the EarlySchool preschool program. Our goal is to accommodate 500 migrant children arriving from Mexico, El Salvador, Guatemala, and Honduras, across various locations in Coastville.

Description of the Project: Coastville is experiencing a significant influx of preschool-aged children from Central America, creating an urgent demand for expanded educational resources. In collaboration with EarlySchool, Pre-Escolar Fantasia aims to address this demand by expanding our existing site and establishing four new sites strategically located across Coastville. This expansion will provide culturally sensitive and inclusive early childhood education to 500 migrant children, fostering a supportive learning environment that promotes their overall development.

Distinctive Approach: Pre-Escolar Fantasia is committed to providing a welcoming and culturally sensitive space for preschoolers from diverse backgrounds. Our existing site has successfully met the unique needs of migrant children, and this expansion will allow us to extend these benefits to an even larger population. Our dedicated team, including key staff members from Mexico, El Salvador, Guatemala, and Honduras, bring firsthand cultural understanding and language proficiency to ensure effective communication and a nurturing environment.

Educational Significance: We believe that investing in the early development of these young minds is crucial for their future success. The expansion of Pre-Escolar Fantasia's EarlySchool preschool program will not only provide high-quality early childhood education but also contribute to the positive development of the entire migrant community. Our program empowers children to become conduits for language acquisition within their families, aiding in the successful integration of parents into the community.

Funding Request: We are seeking a grant of $1.5 million to support the expansion of Pre-Escolar Fantasia's EarlySchool preschool program. This funding will cover expanding our current site and establishing four new sites, staffing needs, curriculum development, and resources required for a successful learning environment. The breakdown of the budget is as follows:

Site establishment: $800,000

Staffing and training: $300,000

Curriculum development: $200,000

Learning resources: $200,000

Community Support: We are pleased to share that we have garnered strong community support for this expansion initiative. Local businesses and organizations have expressed their commitment to providing in-kind support, including classroom equipment and consumables, further emphasizing the community's dedication to the success of this program.

Success of our initiative will immediately help to improve the lives of our children and their families. With the new skills learned, the future will be brighter for generations.

We believe that the expansion of Pre-Escolar Fantasia's EarlySchool preschool program aligns with the mission and goals of Gelt4Good Foundation. We would be grateful for the opportunity to discuss this proposal further and explore how this initiative can positively impact the lives of migrant children in Coastville.

Thank you for considering our Letter of Inquiry. We look forward to the possibility of working together to make a lasting impact on the education of migrant children, and their families and the community for now and the future,

Sincérele,

Vida Esperanza

Executive Director

Vida@Pre-Escolar.org

Pre-Escolar Fantasia

LIBBY HIKIND

V: The Future of AI and Grant Writing

AI can help you write grants. I decided to use the development of an LOI, as an example to teach you how to work with artificial intelligence.

Before you begin with AI, you need to do the mapping. An LOI is a mini grant application. You must have a program and a budget. Do not let AI plan a program that the organization has not agreed to.

Your LOI does not have to be filled with all the details. An LOI is more of a general overall plan.

AI will help you with language as it is a language model. It will help you to say it better, However, you must read what you copy very carefully.

How I prompted ChatGPT to write a sample LOI.

I took an old LOI I had in my files from 5 years ago. I wanted to teach Chat the format that I wanted, and I gave her the first prompt. Yes, I said "her" because I think of Chat as an extension of myself when we work together. When prompting Chat of what I want to include, I do not have to write perfect English. It just needs to be clear and direct.

I have listed the main prompts given to Chat. I used poor English purposely, to demonstrate.

"Take this information from a previous LOI and make it for a preschool program serving immigrant children."

I pasted into *chat.openai.com* a complete, previously written LOI. I want to note that the LOI that I pasted in was a page of answers to questions. The original LOI was an online fill in application with space constraints. It was from a dance studio company applying for a grant from a musical instrument company.

What I received was a perfectly formatted LOI with subheadings. However, the content of the LOI was combined with everything from before. I needed the information updated.

My next prompt was: "Change it so that the request is to add a new classroom for preschool children arriving from Mexico, El Salvador, Guatemala, and Honduras - remove all dance and musical instruments."

It was getting better, but the original LOI mentioned a person's name and used his experience to show organizational capacity with the dance company.

"Remove the Mr. Mayfield and make it a woman who migrated with a child 20 years ago."

And Chat did a genuinely nice job of doing that, too.

My next prompt was: "Include that key staff at the facility come from these countries and when selecting new staff, you will be looking for bilingual preschool teachers to accommodate the dialect languages of the children."

Following each prompt, I received the full LOI, and I could review it and modify the LOI with what was missing. At this point, the amount of the funding request was missing.

My next prompt was: "Can you include the amount of money you are requesting $300,000 for staffing and parenting education program and that there are already in-kind community support pledges to donate all the classroom equipment and consumables for the first year."

It was written very nicely by Chat. In two separate paragraphs.

My next prompt was: "In opening paragraph, write that you are submitting this LOI in response to [funding source name]'s RFP for Educating the New Migrant Population. Also, somewhere in the LOI add how we believe that education begins in preschool years and how children speaking English help the adults in the family acclimate to the unfamiliar environment. Also include a statement that parents can find jobs while children are in preschool."

And my final prompt was: "Include as you know government funded programs are overwhelmed. we are a private preschool and have been serving the Latino community for the last 15 years."

An LOI, letter of intent or inquiry written with AI.

[Your Organization's Name] [Address] [City, State, ZIP Code] [Date]

[Granting Organization's Name] [Granting Organization's Address] [City, State, ZIP Code]

Subject: Letter of Inquiry for New Preschool Classroom Serving Immigrant Children from Mexico, El Salvador, Guatemala, and Honduras - Community Funding Area

Dear [Director at Granting Organization's Name],

I am submitting this Letter of Inquiry in response to [funding source name]'s Request for Proposals (RFP) for Educating the New Migrant Population. Our organization is seeking support to expand our preschool program and better address the unique needs of immigrant children arriving from Mexico, El Salvador, Guatemala, and Honduras. By adding a new classroom, we aim to create a more inclusive and culturally sensitive educational environment for these underserved preschoolers.

Description of the Issue or Problem: Our community is experiencing an influx of preschool-aged children from Mexico, El Salvador, Guatemala, and Honduras, creating a demand for additional classroom space. Currently, our existing facilities are nearing capacity, making it challenging to provide the necessary educational resources and individualized attention to each child.

Distinctive Approach: Our program stands out in its commitment to fostering a welcoming and culturally sensitive space for preschoolers from diverse backgrounds. Key staff members at our facility hail from these countries, bringing firsthand cultural understanding and language proficiency. By adding a new classroom, we can tailor our curriculum to meet the specific needs of children arriving from Mexico, El

Salvador, Guatemala, and Honduras, fostering a supportive learning environment that promotes early childhood development.

Why We Are Well-Suited: Led by a woman who migrated with a child 20 years ago, our all-volunteer program is uniquely equipped to address the challenges faced by immigrant children. In addition to our leader's personal journey as an immigrant, our key staff members come from these countries, providing invaluable cultural insights. When selecting new staff, we prioritize bilingual preschool teachers to accommodate the dialect languages of the children, ensuring effective communication and understanding.

Educational Significance: We believe that education begins in the preschool years, and investing in the early development of these young minds is crucial for their future success. Furthermore, we recognize the positive impact of preschool education on the entire family unit. Children who learn English at an early age often become conduits for language acquisition within their families, helping adults acclimate to the unfamiliar environment.

Parents' Employment Opportunities: Additionally, we understand that parents face challenges in finding employment while caring for their children. Our preschool program serves as a valuable resource by providing a supportive learning environment for children, allowing parents the opportunity to seek employment, further contributing to their successful integration into the community. As you know, government-funded programs are overwhelmed, and our role as a private preschool has been significant in alleviating the strain on public resources. For the past 15 years, we have been proudly serving the Latino community, addressing the unique needs, and fostering a strong foundation for educational success.

Funding Request: We are seeking a grant of $300,000 to support the staffing needs and the implementation of a comprehensive parenting education program. This funding will enable us to hire qualified bilingual preschool teachers, conduct parenting education workshops, and provide the necessary resources to ensure a successful learning environment for the children.

Community Support: We are pleased to share that we have already secured in-kind community support pledges to donate all classroom equipment and consumables for the first year. This demonstrates the strong commitment of our community to the success of this program.

We kindly request your support to help us create a new classroom space that will benefit preschool children arriving from Mexico, El Salvador, Guatemala, and Honduras.

Thank you for considering our proposal. We look forward to the opportunity to discuss this further and explore how our program aligns with the mission and goals of [Granting Organization's Name].

Sincerely,

[Your Name] [Your Title] [Your Contact Information]

The use of AI, Artificial Intelligence

Artificial Intelligence or AI or ChatGPT and a host of others, is a great application that aids in creating a clean writing style. Additionally, it can help with readability.

However, do not let AI plan your program or provide internal organizational data. Plan your program with your Board of Directors and input the data you want displayed.

Never use artificial intelligence to quote sources unless you provide the source and text and place it in a prompt for Chat to include.

You can use Chat as an application to speed up the writing process and organize your data. Use it much the same way as you were using PowerPoint over the last few years as an application to make a presentation.

However, and this is important, all the thoughts, plans, goals, etc., must always be yours.

To use Chat, you need to feed it the information you have a few times until you get it exactly right. Even now when I look at my sample LOI, I realize I left some things out.

I challenge you to copy the sample or some part of it and ask Chat to include the 3 missing parts: dissemination, replicability, and sustainability. When writing an LOI you should mention everything.

Please take the AI challenge and play with Chat.

My book is ending, and your story is beginning.

Congratulations! Now that you have finished reading this book you understand the need to verify your eligibility, what content you need, how to follow directions, and how to use PMF, Passion, Maps and Folders to plan out and write your grant application.

I hope that you understand that while every grant written does not get funded, unfunded grants are still a valuable tool for your organization and your development as a grant writer.

When you identify your errors, and or your omissions you will determine how you might have gained more points. You will also identify the parts that are mostly boilerplate so that you can use them in your next application.

You should continue to look for new funding opportunities on GrantWatch.com where new grants are added, every day.

If you leave yourself enough lead time to review your creative grant application slowly and meticulously, before submitting, success will be within your reach.

We have come full circle. My first foray into grant writing was with word processing and I leave you now with the challenge of AI and how to use it ethically and responsibly.

My last piece of grant writing advice is, "Submit early, but never quickly. Live with your document for a while. Review it entirely and then submit."

I wish you the best of luck in your new grant writing career. And remember: "You got this!"

LIBBY HIKIND

ABOUT THE AUTHOR

Libby Hikind, renowned as the "Queen of Grants," is the Founder and CEO of GrantWatch.com, a prominent grant funding search engine.

With a career spanning over 29 years in the New York City Department of Education, Libby's foray into grant writing began out of necessity as a special education teacher in need of computer equipment for her classroom; and continued at the Brooklyn school district where she successfully secured $11 million in grants, in just two years.

In 1994, Libby took a giant leap forward by establishing her first grant writing agency which published NYCGrantsWatch, a weekly faxed grant newsletter. 2010 marked a pivotal moment in Libby's career as she launched a platform meticulously designed to cater to the needs of grant writers and board members.

GrantWatch.com showcases 7,500 to 8,000 grants across 60 categories, complemented by comprehensive IRS 990 reports. Today, GrantWatch.com is the trailblazer in the grant industry, drawing over 230,000 monthly visitors.

Libby's influence extends beyond her digital ventures. Libby is a wife, mother, grandmother, and great-grandmother.

She has been a featured guest on TV news segments, podcasts, and radio shows, including appearances on *Bloom TV* and *Lifestyle Today*. She has also been an invited guest speaker at nonprofit and C-Suite conferences from Florida to as far away as Dubai. Her insights are found in notable publications such as *Forbes, Inc*, and *Business Insider*. And now Libby has added the title, author, to her list of accomplishments.

ACKNOWLEDGMENTS

I want to extend my appreciation to the dedicated individuals at GrantWatch who played pivotal roles in the editing of my manuscript.

I extend special thanks to Danika, Jeff, Pamela, Susan, and Lani for their collaborative efforts of proofreading the text and deciphering the publishing directions.

A huge amount of gratitude is owed to my two main editors, Lori, and my husband Jacob. We learned and grew together throughout this process.

I would also like to express my gratitude to Jon Flor for creating the beautiful book cover and to The Fellas Media LLC for their outstanding cover photo.

All your contributions have added immense value to this project, and I am truly thankful for the collective effort and creativity that went into bringing this manuscript to life.

www.ingramcontent.com/pod-product-compliance
Lightning Source LLC
Chambersburg PA
CBHW020311010526
44107CB00001B/65